The Medieval Twelve Days of Christmas

The Medieval Twelve Days of Christmas

A musical pageant of the feast days
between December 25 and January 6
as they were celebrated in England
in the late Middle Ages

by
Karis Crawford

The author is eager to hear about performances of *The Medieval Twelve Days of Christmas*. She welcomes requests for advice as well as success stories. Please email her at CedarParkPress@gmail.com. Photos and videos are most welcome!

Printed in the United States of America

First printing January 2019
For ISBN, see back cover

Contents

Guide to Staging

The Purpose of the Pageant

The Medieval Twelve Days of Christmas is a musical pageant that vividly re-creates the feast days between December 25 and January 6 as they were celebrated in England in the late Middle Ages. The days unfold with brief excerpts from plays, legends, sermons, poems, and liturgies—all from texts available in medieval England. Saints and sinners, wassailers and kings, noblewomen and soldiers make appearances, and a narrator provides a unifying voice. Linking the segments are merry carols and haunting chants from the period, offered by instrumentalists and singers. On the stage, a unique Wheel of Christmastide (depicted on the cover of this book) is rotated to mark the progression of the twelve days. Adults and older children perform and are also the targeted audience for the pageant, which runs about 60 to 80 minutes.

The underpinnings of *The Medieval Twelve Days of Christmas* are clearly religious, based on the celebrations that anchored the season for the medieval Christian church. But the pageant is not intended as a religious ritual or church service. It can be enjoyed by people of all religious traditions—or of no religion—as a historical presentation about one of the world's most beloved festivals. Although the narratives and songs are authentic to the period, the materials have been crafted in Modern English to be easily understood by today's audiences.

Please note that this pageant is based on Christian observances in England in the late Middle Ages, not on the later song about a partridge in a pear tree!

The Celebrations

December 25	The Feast of the Nativity of Jesus, Christmas Day
December 26	The Feast of St Stephen
December 27	The Feast of St John the Evangelist
December 28	The Feast of the Holy Innocents
December 29	The Feast of St Thomas Becket
December 30	The Sixth Day in the Octave of Christmas
December 31	The Feast of St Sylvester
January 1	The Feast of the Naming of Jesus and New Year's Day
January 2	Weekday (Feria) of the Christmas Season
January 3	Weekday (Feria) of the Christmas Season
January 4	Weekday (Feria) of the Christmas Season
January 5	The Vigil of the Epiphany, Twelfth Night
January 6	The Feast of the Epiphany

How are the twelve days of the season counted? It varies. Some sources make Christmas Day, December 25, the first day and end the twelve days on the night of January 5, Twelfth Night. Other sources make St Stephen's Day, December 26, the first day and end the twelve days on Epiphany, January 6. In this pageant, both Christmas Day, December 25, and Epiphany, January 6, are presented, so audience members are free to count the days however they like. The pageant is not set in any particular year but offers a general view of traditions and songs available in England in the later Middle Ages—about the 14th and 15th centuries. Some liturgical selections were written in the early Middle Ages but continued to be used in subsequent centuries.

For those not familiar with Christian liturgy, it's helpful to know that the celebrations of the Christmas season commemorate events from many different centuries. Some of the Christmastide feast days are chronologically associated with the birth of Jesus. For example, Epiphany (January 6) marks the coming of the Wise Men to pay homage to the infant Jesus in 1st-century Bethlehem. Other feast days refer to events after the death of Jesus or much later. For example, Stephen (December 26) was an early Christian martyr, Sylvester (December 31) was a 4th-century pope, and Thomas Becket (December 29) was an archbishop in 12th-century Britain. People in the Middle Ages did not find this leaping of centuries incongruous.

Audience and Performance Dates

The Medieval Twelve Days of Christmas is a family-friendly pageant that is appropriate for audiences of upper-elementary-school age through adult. Although martyrdoms are commemorated on December 26, 28, and 29, the dramatic excerpts used in the pageant are not graphically violent. (The actual medieval presentations have been toned down.)

Almost all components of the pageant have been translated into Modern English from the original Latin or Middle English. A few songs that mix Latin and Middle English (for December 31, January 1, and January 5) would lose a lot of their appeal if sung in translation. For these, the Singers use the original languages, and Modern English translations are provided for use in the printed program. See **Program for Audience**, below.

The Medieval Twelve Days of Christmas reveals the richness of the entire Christmas season, not just the gift-giving day of December 25 in modern culture. So the pageant will likely be more meaningful to the audience if it's presented on a date between December 26 and January 6, when the significance of the post-Christmas feast days is stronger. That said, *The Medieval Twelve Days of Christmas* can be performed any time during the winter holidays.

Presenting Organization

Churches, church-affiliated high schools and colleges, living history groups, early music ensembles, and local theater companies are all possible presenting organizations for *The Medieval Twelve Days of Christmas*. Directors who are accustomed to scripts for stage plays will find the materials for this pageant somewhat different. The script for *The Medieval Twelve Days of Christmas* is divided into segments, by days, rather than into acts and scenes. A **Summary Grid of the Script** gives a handy overview of these segments, laying out the texts, music, and cast members for each. Staging instructions that are set out in this introductory **Guide to Staging** are reiterated in each segment, to assist organizations that have less experience in theatrical presentations. Descriptive text that is very helpful for audience understanding appears in the **Program for Audience** section, below.

Permission is granted to the purchasers of this book to stage *The Medieval Twelve Days of Christmas* pageant without payment of royalty, provided that Karis Crawford is credited as the author in advertising and in programs provided to the audience.

Performers

The Medieval Twelve Days of Christmas has been written for performance by a volunteer cast of adults, teens, and older children. It's assumed that the performers will be amateur actors, singers, and instrumentalists who have had little or no training in theater. Since the memorizing of lines can be daunting for non-professionals, the script has been designed so that many characters do not speak or speak only a few lines. Some actors with speaking parts may be able to read their lines from the surfaces of the props that they carry. Family groups can be encouraged to volunteer for the cast, with children over about the age of ten taking on non-speaking roles such as Wassailers or St John's Helpers. If experienced performers are available, the production can, of course, be much more polished.

As is noted in the section below on **Casting Strategies**, some roles can be assumed by either males or females, and some roles can be doubled so that the pageant can be presented with fewer actors. *The Medieval Twelve Days of Christmas* was originally staged in a large church in Ann Arbor, Michigan, with several dozen church members performing and assisting backstage. For more information on **Singers** and **Instrumentalists**, see below.

Performance Site and Lighting

The script for *The Medieval Twelve Days of Christmas* calls for a performance space with three aisles (a central aisle and two side aisles), but sites with one or two aisles can also work fine. If the performance takes place in a large open room, it's helpful to have a raised stage or platform in front of the audience. If the performance takes place in a church, this stage might be the altar area. In any case, the stage should have an entry on each side and steps leading down to the audience level. Near the front of the performance space, at stage left but at audience level, seating should be reserved for the Instrumentalists and the Singers. No theater curtain is used for *The Medieval Twelve Days of Christmas*. If the performance takes place in an auditorium with a traditional stage, the curtain should remain open for the entire performance, to emphasize the continuity of the segments.

Directors should feel free to modify the stage directions in the script to suit the physical configurations of their performance site. For example, if there is no backstage area, screens might be erected for characters who are waiting to enter. Most performance sites will need three persons to cue actors for their entrances (backstage right, backstage left, and lobby).

It's assumed that many performance sites for *The Medieval Twelve Days of Christmas* will not have a stage lighting system. The script includes a few optional spotlighting suggestions, but general overhead lighting of the stage area (or front of the church) can illuminate most of the action. The script indicates when stage lights and house lights should be turned up and down. Even in the absence of full stage lighting, the Director should designate a person to handle lights. This might be the Stage Manager.

For the December 26 and January 6 segments, the Director may choose to have the audience join in on carols. If this option is chosen, it's important that the house lights (in the audience area) be up during the singing. In addition, one essential lighting effect takes place in the December 29 segment. At the moment that Thomas Becket is attacked, all lights on the stage and in the audience are extinguished (blackout), so that the actor playing Becket can move out of view of the audience.

Music

Carols and chants from the Middle Ages set the scenes and provide the transitions for *The Medieval Twelve Days of Christmas* pageant. Musical selections have been carefully chosen to balance authenticity to the medieval period with singability by 21st-century vocalists.

The script of the pageant coordinates with music and lyrics in *The New Oxford Book of Carols*, edited by Hugh Keyte and Andrew Parrott, with associate editor Clifford Bartlett (Oxford University Press, 1992). This widely available book is a definitive edition, with extensive source and performance notes. Because *The New Oxford Book of Carols* is such a comprehensive single resource, **music scores are not included with the script**

of *The Medieval Twelve Days of Christmas*. Please observe copyright laws in using music.

The music for the December 29 segment is the only selection in *The Medieval Twelve Days of Christmas* that is not found in *The New Oxford Book of Carols*. This music is the well-known 15th-century tune *Agincourt*, which is found in the hymnals of most major Christian denominations. (See hymnary.org for a list of the hymnals in which it is available, often with the title "O love, how deep, how broad, how high.") The lyrics for use with the *Agincourt* tune, specific to Thomas Becket, are in the pageant script.

Ideally, a Music Director will be designated to organize instrumental accompaniments, to oversee rehearsals of the Singers and the Instrumentalists, and to conduct at the performance. Initial musical rehearsals may be separate from rehearsals of the dramatic segments of the pageant, but for at least the dress rehearsal all musicians and actors should be present, so that the continuity of the production can be smoothed.
It's possible for the audience to sing along on two of the best-known of surviving medieval carols: "Of the Father's heart begotten" (December 26) and "On this day earth shall ring" (January 6). These carols are often included in the hymnals of major Christian denominations. If the pageant is presented in a church setting where hymnals are available, the audience can be directed to the appropriate number in the hymnals. Otherwise, the texts for these carols can be included in the printed program distributed to the audience members. See **Program for Audience**, below.

The language that the Singers use varies:

- For some musical selections, both the original language (Latin or Middle English) and the metrical Modern English version can be found in *The New Oxford Book of Carols*. In these cases (December 25 opening chant; end carols on December 26, December 27, and January 6), the choice of language falls to the Director or the Music Director.
- For the musical selections at the end of the December 25 and January 2/3/4 segments, no metrical Modern English version appears in *The New Oxford Book of Carols*, so original metrical translations are provided in the pageant script for the Singers.
- The carols at the end of the December 31 and January 1 segments and the refrain at the end of the January 5 segment do not adapt well to translation. These carols should be sung in the original languages. A literal translation is provided for use in the printed program for the audience. See **Program for Audience**, below.
- The "Coventry Carol" at the end of the December 28 segment has fairly simple vocabulary and can be sung in the original Middle English.

The Music Director will want to tailor the instrumental components of the songs based on the nature of the song and on the Instrumentalists available for the performance. Here are some suggestions:

- The opening chant for December 25, "Come, thou redeemer of the earth," should be unaccompanied but might include the sounding of a triangle or bell to mark the end of each verse.
- The vocals of the plaintive "Coventry Carol" on December 28 might be accompanied quietly by a guitar or lute.
- The meditative words of "Ther is no rose of swych vertu" for January 2/3/4 would work well with a recorder accompaniment.
- Rollicking carols (such as "Christmastime at last is here" on December 25, "Make we joye nowe in this fest" on January 1, and "Gaudete" on January 5) call for full instrumental accompaniment, possibly including drum.
- If the audience is joining the Singers on the carols for the December 26 and January 6 segments, strong instrumental accompaniment should guide the audience in singing.
- On some musical selections, the Music Director may want to experiment with bass drones, but this will depend on the performance abilities of the Instrumentalists available.
- Between all the segments of the pageant, the Wassailers will be turning the Wheel of Christmastide (see **Scenery and Props**, below). **This action must always have musical accompaniment.** Since the vocal selections may end before the Wassailers have finished their frolicking, the Instrumentalists should repeat the melody line of the selection just ended, without vocals, until the Wassailers finish their actions and exit.

Several of the musical selections in *The Medieval Twelve Days of Christmas* have been recorded on CD by the excellent vocal group The Sixteen, conducted by Harry Christophers (thesixteen.com). Other performances are readily available on YouTube, but be cautious in adopting pronunciations from these videos. In particular, numerous rock groups have performed and recorded the popular "Gaudete," used at the end of the January 5 segment, with erratic pronunciation of the Latin. Ecclesiastical pronunciation of Latin—also called "church pronunciation"—is preferred by classical musicians. Many guides can be found online. For Middle English pronunciation, the guide in *The New Oxford Book of Carols*, Appendix 1, is reliable.

Singers

A minimum of six and a maximum of about twelve vocalists, all of whom are comfortable with singing unaccompanied chant and basic melodies, should be recruited for the Singers. It's desirable but not essential that these vocalists also be able to sing two-part or three-part harmony. The Singers can be treble or bass voices or a mix. Singing on the octave is fine. Older children who have choir experience can certainly be included among the Singers. For songs not specifically unison, there can be considerable latitude in assigning the melody line. If there is no Music Director, one member of the Singers should be designated as the lead for the group.

In rehearsals, the Singers will want to practice where notes line up with lyrics, especially when singing unfamiliar Latin words. Absolute adherence to the alignment in *The New Oxford Book of Carols* is not required—the actual medieval practice is often unclear. In some of the carols with refrains, the Music Director may want to feature a small group of vocalists on the verses and the entire group of vocalists on the refrains, as seems to have been the medieval practice. Note that the Singers should lead with the melody for the two carols that the audience may be asked to join in on.

Instruments and Instrumentalists

The non-chant musical selections of the pageant should be accompanied by instruments. If there is no Music Director, one Instrumentalist should be designated as the lead for the group, to cue entrances and set tempos.

If the group has access to reproductions of medieval instruments and to musicians skilled in playing them, the performance can be exceptionally authentic! However, most groups performing *The Medieval Twelve Days of Christmas* will not have such access.

The **bare minimum instruments** needed are

- **Strings:** guitar or lute
- **Winds:** flute or soprano recorder
- **Percussion:** hand drum (frame drum), cymbals (can be toy cymbals), bell, tambourine, two kazoos

If your group can pull together these instruments—and people who can play them—you can stage a performance of *The Medieval Twelve Days of Christmas*. For example, you could get by with four instrumentalists: one guitarist, one recorder player, and two percussionists. A good source for reasonably priced instruments is West Music (westmusic.com).

If you are able to gather a **larger ensemble**, several instruments can work:

- **Strings:** Guitar, lute, harp, and hammered dulcimer. Violin, viola, and cello are also fine, with cello on the bass line. Some modern lutes and hammered dulcimers are similar to the medieval versions. Other medieval string instruments included the plucked or struck gittern and psaltery, and the bowed rebec and vielle.

- **Winds:** Recorder in all its sizes, plus clarinet. Flute, oboe, and bassoon are also fine, with bassoon on the bass line. The modern recorder is similar to the medieval recorder. Medieval wind instruments also included the shawm and gemshorn.
- **Percussion:** Hand drum (frame drum), cymbals, finger cymbals, bells, triangle, and tambourine, all of which were available in some form during the late Middle Ages. The hand drum (frame drum) can be played with a soft mallet if desired. Clapping of hands and stomping of feet can also be employed.

For ideas about instrumentation, the Music Director may want to listen to recordings of medieval Christmas music by groups such as Ensemble Galilei (egmusic.com).

Some instruments should be **avoided**:

- Keyboard instruments such as piano and organ should **not** be used. Although a small portable organ was in use during the Middle Ages, its sound is difficult to reproduce on a large modern pipe organ, which is too loud for the medieval music selections.
- Brass instruments should **not** be used, since they can drown out the vocalists.
- Snare drums, drumsticks, and hi-hat cymbals should **not** be used.

For **sound effects** in the pageant, four specific instruments are needed:

- **Finger cymbals or a bell or a triangle** to mark the birth of Jesus in the December 25 segment.
- A **hand drum and cymbals** for the death of Thomas Becket in the December 29 segment. Toy cymbals can be used.
- Two **kazoos** for a mock fanfare before the entrance of the Green Knight in the January 1 segment.
- A **hand drum** for the exit of Stephen in the December 26 segment and for the entry of the three Wise Men in the January 6 segment.

Scenery and Props

The Medieval Twelve Days of Christmas requires no background scenery. A reading stand with a light should be placed downstage right, with two chairs behind it, during the entire performance. In a church setting, the reading stand might be the fixed lectern near the altar. If a sound system is available, a microphone should be used at the reading stand by the Narrator and by the Reader. Microphones are generally not needed for other cast members if they are directed to speak loudly.

The most critical prop is the **Wheel of Christmastide**. This is a large, upright, rotating disk with the dates of the days of Christmas painted or affixed on it. The Wheel of

Christmastide remains visible throughout the pageant of *The Medieval Twelve Days of Christmas.* It can be made of stiff, heavy cardboard or thin plywood and should be about three feet in diameter for good visibility by the audience. The Wheel is divided into twelve equal wedges, radiating from the center and painted in alternating colors of deep red and forest green. The dates of the twelve days following Christmas (26, 27, 28, 29, 30, 31, 1, 2, 3, 4, 5, 6) should appear on the outer edges of the twelve wedges, with the tops of the numbers at the outer edge of the Wheel. White numbers stand out best. **See the picture on the cover of this book as a guide for construction.** The font used on the cover is French Script MT.

The Wheel of Christmastide should have a hole in the middle by which it is mounted to a post. This mounting must allow the Wheel to be turned by the Wassailers and then remain stationary when the turning stops. At the top of the post, above the Wheel, a large arrow should point down at the number of the day being presented in the pageant. The post for the Wheel can be quite simple—for example, a fence post stuck into a bucket of concrete, with a large nail for the Wheel to hang on and a piece of burlap to cover the concrete. Or it can be elaborate—for example, a customized lamppost with a weighted base. A large piece of burlap or other rough fabric should cover the entire Wheel of Christmastide at the opening of the pageant and during the December 25 segment.

Another major prop is the **Green Knight puppet**, appearing in the January 1 segment. The head of this puppet, larger than life and painted bright green all over, can be made from papier-mâché and mounted on a piece of vertical wooden furring about five feet in length. Below the head, a three-foot horizontal wooden furring crosspiece serves as the shoulders of the Green Knight. On this crosspiece a bright green robe or piece of cloth should be draped. On cue from the Narrator, a puppeteer holds the Green Knight puppet aloft.

Small props needed for the pageant are listed with each segment and are also summarized here:

- three or four pounds of walnuts in shells
- small woven-wood baskets (may have bells attached; one basket for each of the Wassailers)
- low wooden stool
- 18-inch doll wrapped in plain blanket
- two small logs of wood
- simple wooden pole with shiny star, preferably tin and about a foot across, affixed at the top
- three papier-mâché rocks, about 10-12 inches in diameter, painted gray

- bird and/or animal masks on sticks (one for each Wassailer, to be held up to the face)
- simple wooden pole with a crosspiece at the top to hold a banner depicting an eagle
- scepter (hand-held wand with decorated ball at the tip)
- two scrolls (rolled-up strips of paper, each about a foot wide and two feet long)
- four long swords (can be made from stiff cardboard or thin plywood)
- simple wooden pole with a crosspiece at the top to hold a banner depicting a triple tiara (three-tiered crown)
- scythe (can be made from stiff cardboard or thin plywood)
- six small boxes, wrapped in solid fabric, representing New Year's gifts
- oversized stemmed red rose, made from fabric; if unavailable, a bouquet of regular-sized red fabric roses may be substituted.
- three small decorated boxes representing gold, frankincense, and myrrh

Three of the props used for the December 25 segment (stool, wrapped doll, and pole with star) are reused in the January 6 segment. Two of the four swords used in the December 29 segment are reused in the January 1 segment. The wooden pole that holds the eagle banner in the December 27 segment can be constructed so that it will hold the tiara banner in the December 31 segment. The Stage Manager should handle these changes backstage.

Summary of Characters

Narrator holds the segments together with explanations from the script. He/she sits behind the lectern next to the Reader and rises to speak at the lectern, with no memorized lines. The Narrator should have a clear, distinct speaking voice.

Reader reads passages from medieval texts throughout the pageant. He/she sits behind the lectern next to the Narrator and rises to read at the lectern, with no memorized lines. The Reader should have a clear, distinct speaking voice.

Wassailers, wearing Robin-Hood-style hats, turn the Wheel of Christmastide in between segments of the pageant and sometimes frolic up and down the aisles on their way to this task. At the end of the December 29 segment they hold bird/animal masks up to their faces. At the end of the segments for December 31 and January 5, they hand out walnuts from baskets to audience members. Three or four Wassailers, male or female, are needed. They have no speaking lines.

Singers provide the vocals for the musical selections in each segment of the pageant. They have no memorized lines because they have scripts plus copies of *The New Oxford*

Book of Carols. In addition to their singing, the Singers shout out four lines on cue from the Narrator at the end of the December 25 segment. See **Music** and **Singers**, above, for more details.

Instrumentalists provide the musical accompaniments and interludes for the pageant as well as the sound effects. They have no memorized lines because they have scripts plus copies of *The New Oxford Book of Carols.* See **Music** and **Instruments and Instrumentalists**, above, for more details.

Joseph, the frazzled husband of Mary, is usually portrayed as an older man. He appears in the December 25 segment carrying two logs and in the January 6 segment carrying a wooden stool. He has 28 lines to memorize for December 25. Some of these lines may be concealed in the logs.

Mary, the calm mother of Jesus, appears in the December 25 and January 6 segments, both times carrying a wrapped doll. She has 21 lines to memorize for December 25 and 6 lines to memorize for January 6. These lines may be concealed in the doll blanket. In the January 2/3/4 segment, she carries a large red fabric rose. She has no lines for this segment.

Pole Bearer, who walks in a stately manner, appears in the December 25, December 27, December 31, and January 6 segments, with different poles. The Pole Bearer can be male or female. He/she has no speaking lines.

Stephen, the first martyr of the Christian era, is celebrated in the December 26 segment. He has 2 lines to memorize.

Rock Pelter A, Rock Pelter B, and Rock Pelter C, who stone Stephen, each carry a large rock. These three non-speaking actors appear in the December 26 segment.

John, the evangelist and friend of Jesus, is portrayed in his great old age in the December 27 segment. John has Helpers holding his arms on either side to walk. He has 3 lines to memorize.

Helper A, Helper B, and Helper C, who assist John as he walks on and off the stage, appear in the December 27 segment. At least two, but preferably three, Helpers are needed, male or female but dressed as males. One of the Helpers has 1 line to memorize.

Herod, the king of Judea who was said to have ordered the slaughter of infants, wears a crown and carries a scepter. Herod is portrayed as an angry tyrant. He has 32 lines to memorize for the December 28 segment, and these lines cannot easily be concealed in a prop.

Counselor A and Counselor B accompany Herod in the December 28 segment. Counselor A has 11 lines to speak, and Counselor B has 22 lines to speak. However, each Counselor carries a scroll that he refers to in the drama, so the Counselors do not have to memorize their lines.

Thomas Becket, the archbishop of Canterbury who was martyred in the year 1170, appears in the December 29 segment, wearing his archbishop's miter. He has 6 lines to memorize.

Knight A, Knight B, Knight C, and Knight D, who assassinated Thomas Becket in Canterbury Cathedral, appear in the December 29 segment, each carrying a sword. Each Knight has 1 line to memorize.

Sylvester, who was a pope during the 4th century, appears in the December 31 segment, wearing his papal triple tiara (a three-tiered crown). Since Sylvester is associated with Father Time, he is portrayed as an elderly man with a long white beard. He carries a scythe and has no spoken lines.

Arthur, a legendary king of Britain, wears a crown for his appearance in the January 1 segment. On cue from the Narrator, Arthur shouts "Noel" with his entourage.

Guinevere, Arthur's queen, also wears a crown and appears in the January 1 segment. On cue from the Narrator, Guinevere shouts "Noel" with her entourage.

Arthur's Lords (minimum of three actors) accompany Arthur in the January 1 segment. One Lord carries a couple of small fabric-wrapped boxes; two Lords carry swords. On cue from the Narrator, the Lords shout "Noel."

Guinevere's Ladies (minimum of three actors) accompany Guinevere in the January 1 segment, carrying several small fabric-wrapped boxes. On cue from the Narrator, the Ladies shout "Noel."

The Green Knight is a giant puppet, surprising and somewhat fearsome, who appears in the January 1 segment, held aloft by the Puppeteer. See **Scenery and Props** section above for details. The Green Knight has no spoken lines.

Puppeteer is the cast member who holds the Green Knight puppet aloft on cue in the January 1 segment. The Puppeteer, who can be male or female, has no spoken lines.

Caspar, one of the Three Wise Men (Kings) appearing in the January 6 segment, wears a crown and carries a small box that represents gold. He is often depicted as an elderly man. He has 8 lines to memorize, but it's possible to have the lines written on his box.

Melchior, one of the Three Wise Men (Kings) appearing in the January 6 segment, wears a crown and carries a small box that represents frankincense. He is often depicted as a middle-aged man. He has 8 lines to memorize, but it's possible to have the lines written on his box.

Balthasar, one of the Three Wise Men (Kings) appearing in the January 6 segment, wears a crown and carries a small box that represents myrrh. He is often depicted as a young man with dark skin color. He has 8 lines to memorize, but it's possible to have the lines written on his box.

Casting Strategies

Because *The Medieval Twelve Days of Christmas* is presented in distinct segments, some roles can be doubled with minimal costume changes, such as different headgear and the addition or removal of a cape or beard. For doubling to work well, the performance site must allow for actors to move between the backstage area and the lobby without being seen by the audience. Here are a few of the possibilities:

- Rock Pelters A, B, and C (December 26) can double as three of the four Knights (December 29)
- Knights A, B, C, and D (December 29) can double as Lords (January 1)
- Lords (January 1) can double as Caspar, Melchior, and Balthasar (January 6)
- John (December 27) can double as Sylvester (December 31)
- John's Helpers A, B, and C (December 27) can double as Ladies (January 1)
- Pole Bearer (December 25, December 27, December 31, January 6) can double as the Puppeteer (January 1)

Many characters (including the Narrator, Reader, Pole Bearer, Wassailers, and John's Helpers) can be played by either males or females. The Pole Bearer, the Wassailers, and John's Helpers can be played by children over about the age of ten. Non-traditional casting, without consideration for the performers' ethnicity or skin color, is encouraged. These casting strategies can help a director who is working with a small group of volunteer actors.

Costumes

The level of late medieval authenticity in costumes is up to the Director of each production of *The Medieval Twelve Days of Christmas*. Characters can still convey the sense of the medieval period without dressing in authentic costumes. Note that *The Medieval Twelve Days of Christmas* pageant shows how people in the Middle Ages interpreted the Christmas season. For this reason, even if characters are portraying persons from the ancient world (for example, Joseph and Mary), **these characters should dress in medieval fashion**.

Some performance groups may want to rent costumes, but this is certainly not required. Cast members can be encouraged to scour their closets or check secondhand stores for solid-color tunics, robes, capes, leggings, scarves, cowls, and leather boots and sandals, as described below. Everyone should cover up arms, legs, and feet, and most characters should have some sort of headgear. Headgear worn by the actors can help the audience distinguish roles without the use of elaborate costumes. For those who wish to make their own costumes, Simplicity pattern #8587 is recommended. This pattern is called "Renaissance Costume Collection," but the costumes are close to those described below.

Instrumentalists, Joseph, Pole Bearer, Stephen, Rock Pelters, John, and John's Helpers should have simple costumes and no jewelry. Fabrics worn by ordinary people in the Middle Ages were of coarsely woven cloth, such as linen or wool. Since vegetable dyes were used, the colors were muted, neutral earth tones. Shirts and tunics were a natural beige color. Trim was not added, and there were no patterned fabrics. Most people had only one set of clothes, so these were well-worn. The Director can achieve an approximation of the medieval look for the male characters listed here with heavy, dark-colored sweatpants or loose leggings. Female Instrumentalists can wear full-length loose skirts and headscarves. On the top, all can wear a loose shirt with full, long sleeves, in beige or another neutral color. Avoid collars, or else turn collars inside. A loose vest or tunic in a coarse fabric can be worn over the shirt. On the feet, wear dark-colored socks with leather moccasins, sandals, or ankle boots. See **Scenery and Props**, above, for details of the props these actors carry: Joseph carries logs and a wooden stool, the Pole Bearer carries various poles, and the Rock Pelters each carry a large rock.

Wassailers wear felt Robin-Hood-style hats, to distinguish them from other characters. These hats have a broad brim that is turned up at the back and that is pointed like a beak in the front. Male Wassailers dress as in the paragraph above. Female Wassailers may dress as males or may wear full-length loose skirts in place of leggings. The Wassailers hold bird/animal masks up to their faces at the end of the December 29 segment and carry baskets of walnuts to distribute at the end of the December 31 and January 5 segments. The Wassailers may have small bells attached to their baskets or to their persons. See **Scenery and Props**, above, for details.

Knights should ideally have matching tunics over their leggings and matching helmets on their heads. The helmets can be approximated with close-fitting caps of gray fabric, as in Simplicity pattern #8587. Each Knight carries a sword; see **Scenery and Props**, above. Optional: On the front of each tunic can be affixed a cardboard or cloth breastplate with the coat of arms of King Henry II of England (see Wikipedia for images).

Mary has traditionally been dressed in blue. She can wear a full-length loose blue skirt, a loose tunic-type top, and a headscarf made from a large square of cloth folded into a triangle and tied at the nape of the neck. Mary carries a doll wrapped in a plain blanket. See **Scenery and Props**, above.

Herod, Counselors A and B, Sylvester, Arthur, Guinevere, Lords, Ladies, Caspar, Melchior, and Balthasar can be dressed more lavishly than the rest of the cast. The very few wealthy people in the Middle Ages would have had access to fabrics similar to our modern velvet and silk, in various colors. Purple was worn by royalty, and embroidered designs would have been used. The wealthy would also have worn furs as well as jewelry such as belt buckles, finger rings, and brooches to hold capes. Herod, Arthur, Guinevere, and the three Wise Men all wear crowns to indicate their status. Sylvester wears a papal triple tiara (three-level crown); see images on Wikipedia. The crowns can be purchased or made from decorated poster board. The Ladies attending Guinevere wear loose skirts and tunics or robes and can have decorative hats in fabrics such as velvet. Herod carries a scepter; Counselors A and B each carry a scroll; the Lords carry swords or boxes; the Ladies carry boxes; and the three Wise Men each carry a box. See **Scenery and Props**, above.

Thomas Becket wears a plain, long white robe and an archbishop's miter, which is a tall hat tapering up to a point in the front and back, with a deep opening in between. See the image on page 18 for guidance on making a miter from plain white poster board.

Narrator, Reader, Puppeteer, and Singers should wear simple long robes, preferably dark-colored. Some church groups may have available choir robes or clergy vestments that would be suitable. Avoid bright colors.

There are some costume components that all characters should **avoid**:

- Fabrics to avoid: metallic or shiny fabrics, denim, netting, lace, sheers, fluffy fleece, prints of any kind (including animal-skin prints), stripes, checks, plaids, tie-dye, bright colors.
- Styles to avoid: ruffles, cone-shaped hats, visible zippers, visible snaps, bridesmaid or prom dresses, printed tights.
- Shoes to avoid: tennis shoes, athletic shoes, flip-flops, high heels, plastic sandals, men's dress shoes, fluffy slippers, hiking boots, winter boots.
- Accessories to avoid: nail polish, fanny packs, purses, visible rings in piercings other than ears, wristwatches, sunglasses, pagers, phones, chewing gum. If a cast member will trip without corrective eyeglasses, it's better for him/her to wear the eyeglasses.

A Few Scholarly Notes

Scholars of the medieval period will notice that *The Medieval Twelve Days of Christmas* is not meant as an academic text or as a treatise on European celebrations in the Middle Ages. Rather, the pageant is intended as celebratory entertainment for a general, non-academic modern audience.

The script reflects the festive nature of the days following the Christian penitential season of Advent, which started on the fourth Sunday before December 25. The brief selections in the segments of the pageant offer only a tiny sampling of the plays, sermons, poems, liturgies, saints' legends, chants, and carols that were created for the medieval Christmastide, specifically in England in the later Middle Ages. Although January 6 marks the end of *The Medieval Twelve Days of Christmas* pageant, the actual end of the entire Christmas season was Candlemas, the Feast of the Purification of Mary, on February 2, forty days after Christmas.

A few of the carols used in the pageant are preserved in manuscripts dating to the Renaissance, though they are likely medieval in origin. Details of the history of each carol can be found in the footnotes in *The New Oxford Book of Carols*.

About the saints:

- Since *The Medieval Twelve Days of Christmas* depicts historical celebrations, it does not reflect changes in the dates of Christian feast days since the 15th century.
- Minor saints who may have been honored locally in England have been omitted to avoid confusion.
- Sylvester (December 31) is given more emphasis than he likely received in popular culture in England. However, in several countries on the European Continent, December 31 is still called "St Sylvester's Day."
- Some songs written in the Middle Ages expressly for certain saints' days in the Christmas season are extant. However, they have non-catchy tunes, and their scores are not commercially available, so they are not used in the pageant.
- Medieval Christmas celebrations included proportionately many more references to Mary, the mother of Jesus, than are found in this pageant. For instance, songs and sermons recounting the biblical story of the Annunciation of the angel Gabriel to Mary were often folded into Christmas celebrations. To enable modern audiences to focus on Yuletide specifically, these Annunciation components have been greatly reduced in *The Medieval Twelve Days of Christmas*. However, the lovely carol "Ther is no rose of swych vertu" (January 2, 3, and 4) is a nod to the strong medieval tradition of veneration of Mary.

About the languages and the translations:

- Texts used in *The Medieval Twelve Days of Christmas* were originally in either Latin or Middle English. Middle English was the language of England from about the years 1100 to 1500. Some dialects of Middle English are closer to Modern English than others, and some dialects of late Middle English can be intelligible to speakers of Modern English. Hence, a few of the carol lyrics in this pageant can be sung in the original Middle English, as noted in the script. Other carol lyrics are in a mix of Latin and Middle English and don't lend themselves to translation, so these are sung in the original languages, with translations provided for the program distributed to the audience.
- For editions of the medieval texts in the original languages, see **Resources Consulted** below. All editions used as bases for translation are in the public domain. The translations from Latin and Middle English provided in the script are all original to this publication and are quite free, sometimes leaning toward paraphrase.
- The meters, rhymes, and stanza forms of the Middle English poetry are preserved as much as possible. Indentations in stanzas in the script should aid the actors in identifying rhyme patterns. In the selection from *The South English Legendary* (December 27), the irregular lines of about 14 syllables have been smoothed out in the metrical translation. The rich alliteration of the Middle English has occasionally yielded to Modern English clarity. In the selection from *Sir Gawain and the Green Knight* (January 1), no attempt has been made in the translation to replicate the exact rhythmic patterns or caesuras of the long alliterative lines.
- A few archaic words from the original texts (such as "thee," "thou," "ye," "lo," "fie") are retained in the pageant translations to lend a sense of history. An attempt has been made to make the language of the translations slightly more inclusive, even though this was not a concept that would have been understood in the Middle Ages. Thus, for example, "as men shall see" has been translated "as all shall see," but words such as "mankind" do remain in the script.
- Some cultural aspects of medieval Christmas celebrations have been modified for modern audiences. For example, extensive medieval accounts of miracles performed by the saints celebrated in *The Medieval Twelve Days of Christmas* have been omitted. In the selection of excerpts, anti-Semitic components, especially in the story of Herod and the Holy Innocents, have been avoided.

How to Make a Miter for Archbishop Thomas Becket (December 29)

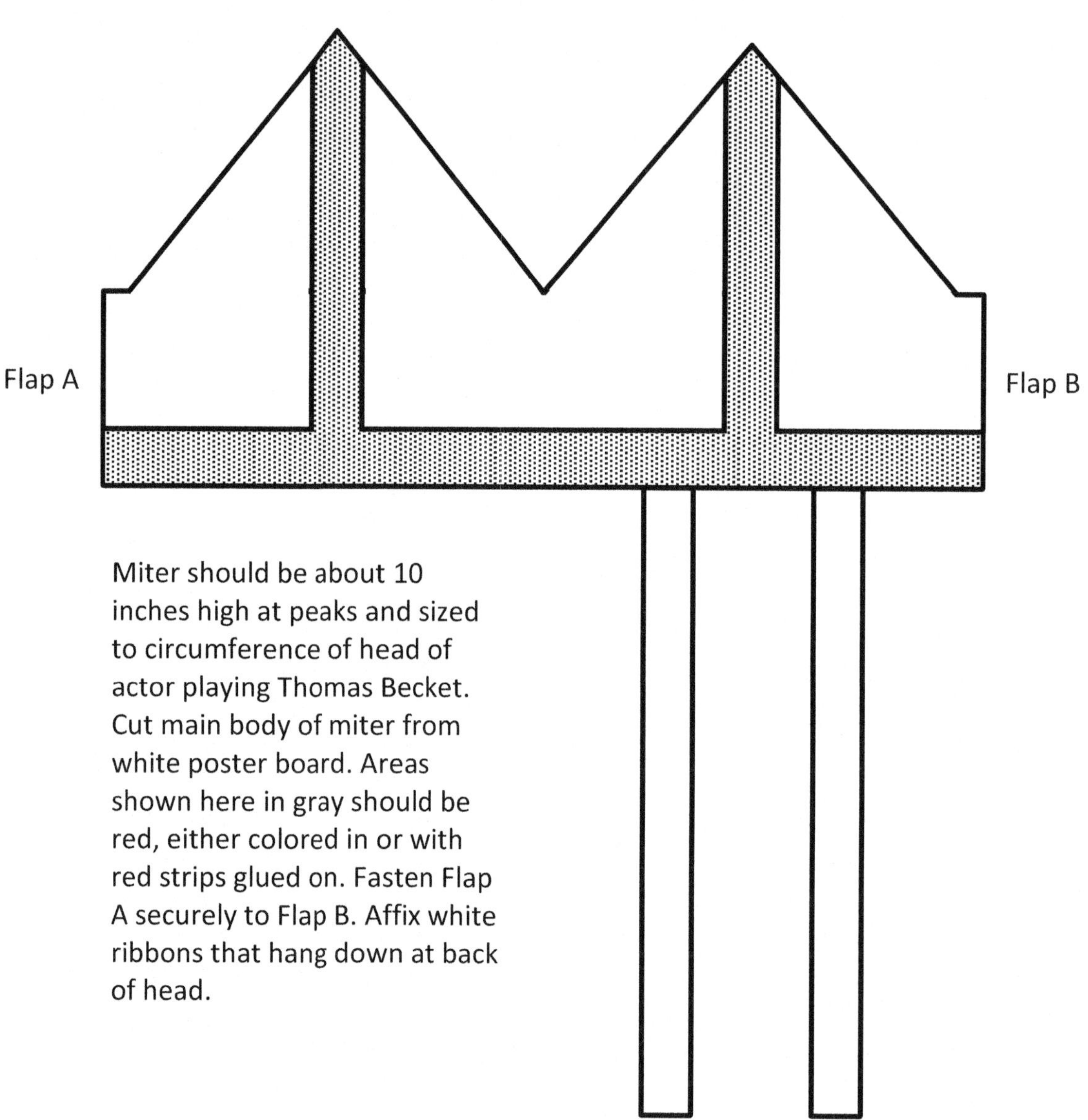

Miter should be about 10 inches high at peaks and sized to circumference of head of actor playing Thomas Becket. Cut main body of miter from white poster board. Areas shown here in gray should be red, either colored in or with red strips glued on. Fasten Flap A securely to Flap B. Affix white ribbons that hang down at back of head.

Program for Audience

The printed program that is distributed to audience members at performances of *The Medieval Twelve Days of Christmas* is an important component for audience understanding of the pageant. It includes an explanation of each segment of the pageant, plus Modern English translations of any Latin and difficult Middle English songs called for in the **Script of the Pageant**, below. If the Director chooses to use additional Latin lyrics, Modern English translations from *The New Oxford Book of Carols* can be added to this text. The text for the program, which may be reproduced, follows. Note that the optional elements, which appear in square brackets, will need to be completed or deleted.

The Medieval Twelve Days of Christmas

A musical pageant of the feast days between December 25 and January 6 as they were celebrated in England in the late Middle Ages

by
Karis Crawford

After the Christian penitential season of Advent, the twelve days of Christmas, from December 25 to January 6, were especially festive in the Middle Ages. Certain days had special celebrations. These feasts of Christmastide commemorated events around the birth of Jesus and also events from other centuries.

December 25 • The Feast of the Nativity of Jesus, Christmas Day

- **Chant—**"Come, thou redeemer of the earth" is a chant used on Christmas Eve at Vespers, the evening service in the Sarum Liturgy of the Hours. This liturgy in Latin is a set of psalms, readings, hymns, and prayers for regular times during each day, especially in monasteries and convents. "Sarum" is the version that was used in England in the Middle Ages. The text of this chant was composed by St Ambrose in the 4th century.
- **Reading—**The opening words were used on Christmas Day at Matins, the night service.

- **Excerpt from a Nativity Play**—This dramatization of the birth of Jesus is from a 15th-century manuscript of plays that were performed in York, England. In many cities in England, biblical stories, called "mystery" plays, were presented by artisan guilds and other performers in the later Middle Ages.
- **Reading**—The reading about the shepherds seeing Jesus in the manger is from Lauds, the dawn service, for Christmas Day.
- **Carol**—"Christmastime at last is here" has been translated from the Latin "Feste dies agitur," a 13th-century English carol.
- **Poem**—"Welcome Yule," from an early 15th-century manuscript, is possibly by John Audelay. It mentions many of the upcoming feast days (including those of Stephen, John, the Holy Innocents, and Thomas Becket) and the celebration of the New Year.

December 26 • The Feast of St Stephen

- **The Wheel of Christmastide**—In the Middle Ages, the circle was a powerful symbol—of the movement of time, of changing fortunes, and of eternity. The Wheel of Christmastide is unique to this pageant.
- **Sermon Excerpt**—The story of Stephen, based on the biblical account, is from the writings of the 14th-century English priest John Mirk, whose book of ready-made sermons for the church year was very popular.
- **Sermon Excerpt**—The poetic section of a sermon by the 6th-century bishop Fulgentius is from the Sarum Liturgy of the Hours for December 26.
- **Carol**—"Of the Father's heart begotten" is one of the oldest surviving Christmas carols. The words are by the 4th-century poet Prudentius, and the tune played here is based on one from the 11th century. [Optional: **Please join in singing** #XXX from the hymnal.]

December 27 • The Feast of St John the Evangelist

- **Excerpt from a Saint's Life**—The rhyming verse about John, the beloved friend of Jesus, is from the 14th-century *South English Legendary*, a lengthy Middle English book of saints' lives.
- **Reading**—The story of John in his old age was well known in the Middle Ages. This 4th-century text, from the writings of St Jerome, is used in the Sarum Liturgy of the Hours for December 27.
- **Carol**—"Unto us is born a son" is from a 14th-century manuscript. One of the verses refers to the story of Herod, which will be presented on December 28.

December 28 • The Feast of the Holy Innocents

- **Sermon Excerpt**—The account from a 13th-century English sermon is based on the biblical story. It tells us that the authorities in Judea, in an attempt to kill the infant Jesus, ordered the deaths of male children, who were known as the Holy

Innocents. In England, December 28 was "Childermas," and in some places a young boy was selected to play the role of bishop for the day.

- **Excerpt from a Herod Play**—This brief excerpt is from the cycle of plays possibly performed in Wakefield, England, in the late Middle Ages. In medieval literature, King Herod was portrayed as a crazed tyrant. References to prophecies about the birth of Jesus were common, with snatches of Latin mixed into the verse and then translated.
- **Carol**—The late medieval "Coventry Carol" was sung in conjunction with the performance of a play about the Holy Innocents in Coventry, England. It is the lament of the mothers of the slain children of Judea.

December 29 • The Feast of St Thomas Becket

- **Excerpt from Martyrdom of Becket**—On December 29, 1170, Thomas Becket, the archbishop of Canterbury, was assassinated in his cathedral. This excerpt from an eyewitness account by Edward Grim is translated from the Latin. The death of Becket shocked all of Europe and made Canterbury, England, a major pilgrimage destination.
- **Carol**—The lyrics of this tribute to Becket are adapted from a 15th-century song and are sung to a well-known 15th-century tune.
- **Wassailers**—It was a practice in medieval England to celebrate Christmastide by wearing bird and animal masks, mainly on the evenings of December 25 and December 29.

December 30 • The Sixth Day in the Octave of Christmas

- All the religious services for the days in the week following Christmas, called "the octave," circled back to the birth of Jesus. As we've seen, some days also celebrated specific saints.

December 31 • The Feast of St Sylvester

- **Summary of Legends**—The story of the 4th-century pope Sylvester is adapted from several medieval legends. It illustrates how religious figures could be transformed into secular symbols, as Sylvester was associated with Father Time.
- **Carol**—"Nowel syng we bothe al and som" is from a 15th-century manuscript. It is sung in a mix of Middle English and Latin. Translation:
  Refrain: We sing Noel, one and all, now that the king of peace has come.
  —It has come to pass in love and joy that Christ has now planned his grace for us, and with his body has saved us for eternal life, one and all. *Refrain.*
  —A boy has been born, sent to us. He saved us for eternal life, rescued us from harm. Otherwise we would have suffered woe, one and all. *Refrain.*
  —Glory always to you, O Lord, and joy. May God guide us toward his grace, so that we do not lose the reward of heaven, one and all. *Refrain.*

January 1 • The Feast of the Naming of Jesus, New Year's Day

- **Excerpt from *Sir Gawain and the Green Knight*—**This long anonymous poem is from the northwest of England in the late 14th century. It opens with a merry New Year's Day celebration at the court of the legendary King Arthur, when a marvelous adventure with the giant Green Knight begins. In folklore, a green man was a symbol of seasonal renewal that was viewed as compatible with Christianity.
- **Carol—**"Make we joye nowe in this fest" is another 15th-century song that mixes Middle English and Latin lines. Translation:
  Refrain: Let us be joyful now at this feast celebrating the birth of Christ.
  —The only son of the Father has come to us from a maiden. Let us sing, saying, "Welcome! O come, savior of the nations." *Refrain.*
  —May every era acknowledge that a bright star caused three kings to come with gifts, seeking the Word made flesh. *Refrain.*
  —Mary conceived in her womb, and the Holy Spirit was truly with her. In Bethlehem is born the one who shares the light of the Father. *Refrain.*
  —O light of the holy Trinity, he lay between an ox and an ass. His mother was a noble maiden. Glory to you, O Lord! *Refrain.*

January 2, 3, and 4 • Weekdays (Feriae) of the Christmas Season

- **Carol—**"There is no rose of such virtue" is a 15th-century song that compares Mary, the mother of Jesus, to a perfect rose.

January 5 • The Vigil of the Epiphany, Twelfth Night

- **Reading—**Throughout the twelve days of Christmas, the Sarum Liturgy of the Hours looks back to the Feast of the Nativity of Jesus, Christmas Day.
- **Summary of Traditions—**Wassailing, the Yule Log, bonfires, and the blessing of orchards were common at Christmastide in medieval England.
- **Carol—**"Gaudete" is a late medieval song in which the audience is exhorted by the refrain, which can be translated from the Latin as "Rejoice! Rejoice! Christ is born of the virgin Mary! Rejoice!"

January 6 • The Feast of the Epiphany

- **Reading—**The poem by Prudentius, from the Sarum Liturgy of the Hours, is about the gifts of the Three Kings or Wise Men. It illustrates the medieval fascination with symbolism and layered meanings. Gold honors Jesus as a king, frankincense honors his divinity, and myrrh points ahead to Easter, when women will come to his tomb to anoint his body.
- **Excerpt from Three Kings Play—**This passage, from a late-15th-century play, was probably written near Peterborough, England.

- **Carol**—In the late medieval carol "On this day earth shall ring," the Latin refrain is the song of the angels at the birth of Jesus: "Therefore, glory to God in the highest." [Optional: **Please join in singing** #XXX from the hymnal.]

Most of the songs heard in *The Medieval Twelve Days of Christmas* appear in *The New Oxford Book of Carols*, edited by Hugh Keyte and Andrew Parrott, with associate editor Clifford Bartlett (Oxford University Press, 1992).

[Insert credits for presenting organization, Director, Music Director, cast, musicians, and crew.]

(END OF PROGRAM FOR AUDIENCE)

A **Summary Grid of the Script** is provided on the following pages.

Summary Grid of the Script

Day	*Feast*	*Texts*	*Music*	*Cast Appearing*
		• ***All medieval texts are excerpts, translated into Modern English.*** • ***Texts are narrated by Narrator, read by Reader, or spoken by performers.***	• ***One song is sung at the end of each day, plus one at the beginning of December 25.*** • ***NOBC = The New Oxford Book of Carols***	***NOTE: For every segment, Reader, Narrator, Wassailers, Singers, and Instrumentalists are also onstage.***
December 25	Nativity of Jesus, Christmas Day	• Sarum Liturgy of the Hours • York Nativity play (15th century) • Sarum Liturgy of the Hours • Poem, possibly by John Audelay (15th century)	***At beginning:*** "Come, thou redeemer of the earth," *NOBC* #2, v 1, 6, 7, & 8, in Modern English or Latin (4th century) ***At end:*** "Christmastime at last is here," *NOBC* #6 ("Feste dies agitur"), v 1, 2, & 3, using Modern English in script (13th century)	• Joseph • Mary • Pole Bearer
December 26	St Stephen	• John Mirk sermon (14th century) • St Fulgentius sermon (6th century, from Sarum Liturgy of the Hours)	"Of the Father's heart begotten," *NOBC* #19 version II, v 1, 4, & 5, in Modern English (4th century); optional audience singing	• Stephen • Rock Pelters A, B, and C
December 27	St John the Evangelist	• *South English Legendary* (14th century) • Reading from St Jerome (4th century, from Sarum Liturgy of the Hours)	"Unto us is born a son," *NOBC* #21, v 1, 3, & 5, in Modern English (14th century)	• John • Helpers A, B, and C • Pole Bearer
December 28	Holy Innocents	• Sermon from Kent (14th century) • Towneley Herod play (15th century)	"Coventry Carol," *NOBC* #40, v 1, 2, & 3, in Middle English (15th/16th century)	• Herod • Counselors A and B
December 29	St Thomas Becket	• Narration about King Henry II and Becket • Account of martyrdom by Edward Grim (12th century)	"Song of St Thomas Becket," v 1, 2, & 3, to the tune *Agincourt*; see script for Modern English lyrics (15th century)	• Thomas Becket • Knights A, B, C, and D

Day	***Feast***	***Texts***	***Music***	***Cast Appearing***
December 30	6th Day in the Octave of Christmas		"Song of St Thomas Becket," v 1, 2, & 3, to the tune *Agincourt*; see script for Modern English lyrics (15th century)	
December 31	St Sylvester	• Narration of legends about 4th-century Sylvester and Father Time	"Nowel syng we bothe al and som," *NOBC* #34, v 1, 3, & 5, in Middle English and Latin (15th century)	• Sylvester • Pole Bearer
January 1	Name Day of Jesus and New Year's Day	• *Sir Gawain and the Green Knight* (14th century)	"Make we joye nowe in this fest," *NOBC* #31, v 1, 2, 4 & 5, in Middle English and Latin (15th century)	• Arthur • Guinevere • Lords • Ladies • Puppeteer with Green Knight puppet
January 2	Weekday (Feria) of the Christmas Season	• Narration about the medieval reverence for Mary	"Ther is no rose of swych vertu," *NOBC* #28, v 1, 2, 3, 4, & 5, in Middle English, or see script for Modern English (15th century)	• Mary
January 3	Weekday (Feria) of the Christmas Season	• Silent procession of Mary	"Ther is no rose of swych vertu," *NOBC* #28, v 1, 2, 3, 4, & 5, in Middle English, or see script for Modern English (15th century)	• Mary
January 4	Weekday (Feria) of the Christmas Season	• Silent procession of Mary, continued	"Ther is no rose of swych vertu," *NOBC* #28, v 1, 2, 3, 4, & 5, in Middle English, or see script for Modern English (15th century)	• Mary
January 5	Vigil of the Epiphany, Twelfth Night	• Sarum Liturgy of the Hours • Narration about the medieval traditions of Twelfth Night	"Gaudete," *NOBC* #51, v 1, 2, & 4; see script for Modern English lyrics, but refrain in Latin (15th/16th century)	
January 6	Epiphany	• Latin poem by Prudentius (4th century, from Sarum Liturgy of the Hours) • Play of the Three Kings (15th century)	"On this day earth shall ring," *NOBC* #20, v 1 & 3, in Modern English (15th/16th century); optional audience singing	• Joseph • Mary • Pole Bearer • Caspar • Melchior • Balthasar

Alternatives for December 31 and January 1 music:

- "Nowell: Owt of your slepe aryse," *NOBC* #33, v 1, 5, & 6, in Middle English
- "Nowell: The borys hede" (The Exeter Boar's Head Carol), *NOBC* #37, v 1, 2, & 3, in Middle English

Script of the Pageant

The Medieval Twelve Days of Christmas

A musical pageant of the feast days
between December 25 and January 6
as they were celebrated in England
in the late Middle Ages

by
Karis Crawford

December 25 Segment
The Feast of the Nativity of Jesus, Christmas Day

Characters for This Segment

Singers, who sing as a group.
Instrumentalists, who accompany the Singers and provide sound effects. They are already seated stage left at audience level when the pageant begins. They should have finger cymbals or a bell or triangle ready to play on cue.
Narrator, whose narration holds the segments together.
Reader, who reads passages from various medieval texts.
Wassailers, who wear Robin-Hood-style hats and turn the Wheel of Christmastide.
Joseph, who is the frazzled husband of Mary; he carries two logs.
Mary, who is the calm mother of Jesus; she carries a wrapped doll.
Pole Bearer, who walks in a stately manner, carrying the star-topped pole.

Setting and Props for This Segment

The stable in Bethlehem where Jesus is born, with no background scenery. The stage has general illumination; the audience is in darkness. If a spotlight is available, it can be used as noted. Props in this segment:

- wooden stool, in place downstage center when the pageant begins
- Wheel of Christmastide, covered with cloth, in place downstage left when the pageant begins
- 18-inch doll wrapped in plain blanket, carried by Mary
- two small logs of wood, carried by Joseph
- simple wooden pole with tin star at least a foot across affixed at the top, carried by Pole Bearer

SINGERS

(Enter two by two from the lobby or back of auditorium, via center aisle, in a slow procession, singing unaccompanied in Latin or Modern English, from music that they carry. Alternatively, Singers can divide up and enter one by one via side aisles. As they sing, they take their places in the seats at audience level, to stage left, near the Instrumentalists. They remain there throughout the performance, standing when they sing.)

"Come, thou redeemer of the earth," #2 in *The New Oxford Book of Carols*, verses 1, 6, 7, and 8.

READER and NARRATOR

(Enter from the lobby or back of auditorium, both slightly behind the Singers. They ascend the steps to the stage. The Narrator sits down behind the lectern. The Reader stands at the lectern. Once the Singers have finished, the Reader speaks.)

READER

(Standing at lectern.)

Today true peace comes down to us from heaven.
Today heaven drips honey upon the entire world.
Today dawns a new redemption,
The deliverance that was announced by the ancient prophets,
Bringing eternal happiness.

(Sits down.)

NARRATOR

(Stands at lectern.)

Events surrounding the birth of Jesus were portrayed in many plays in medieval England. This one is from 15th-century York.

(Sits down.)

MARY

(Enters slowly from backstage left, carrying the swaddled doll that represents the infant Jesus. She sits on the stool downstage center.)

POLE BEARER

(Enters from backstage right, carrying the pole with the star, and stands behind Mary.)

JOSEPH

(Enters from the lobby, via the aisle to stage left, carrying two small logs. When he nears the stage area, before going up the steps to the stage, he stops and turns to the audience, looking upward as he speaks.)

O Lord in heaven, this weather is cold!
The frostiest freeze I ever did feel!
I pray God help those who are old,
And also those who are unwell,
Upon this day.
Dear God, be thou my shelter still,
As best thou may.

(Starts up the steps to the stage. As he speaks, he turns to the audience and shields his eyes. If a spotlight is available, it should be directed on the star at the top of the pole.)

O Lord God, what light is this
That comes a-shining so suddenly?
I cannot tell, as I have bliss.
I'll bring this wood to my Mary,
Then I'll inquire.

(Pauses)

Thanks be to God, the place I see!
I'll light a fire.

(Comes up to the side of Mary.)

My Mary dear, what cheer with thee?

MARY

I'm joyful, Joseph, on this day.

INSTRUMENTALISTS

(Three strikes on triangle or three clangs of finger cymbals or bell.)

JOSEPH

What do I see upon thy knee?

MARY

It is my son, the truth to say,
Who is so mild.

JOSEPH

(Suddenly joyful.)

And I have lived unto this day
To see this child!

(Looking up at the star on the pole.)

I marvel greatly at this light
That shines so brightly in this place!
In truth, it is a wondrous sight!

MARY

God has ordained it of his grace
For this young king.
The star is shining for a space
To mark his coming.

For Scripture long ago foretold
How such a star should rise full high,
And of a maiden should be born
A son that shall our savior be
From cares unkind.
And so, it is my son you see,
As prophesied.

JOSEPH

Now welcome, flower of fairest hue!
I worship thee with all my might!
Hail, maker mine! Hail, Christ Jesú!
Hail, royal king, root of all right!
Hail, Lord of power!
Hail, mighty God and source of light!
Hail, blessed flower!

MARY

Thou gracious savior from on high,
My God, my Lord, my son so free,
Thy handmaid evermore am I,

And to thy service I promise me,
    With heart and mind.
And son, thy blessing I beseech
    Upon mankind.

(Carrying doll, exits stage left slowly with Joseph.)

JOSEPH

(Carrying logs and wooden stool, exits with Mary stage left.)

POLE BEARER

(Carrying pole with star, exits behind Mary and Joseph. The spotlight, if available, follows the star until it is no longer visible to the audience. As the three actors are departing, Narrator and Singers stand.)

NARRATOR

(Stands at lectern.)

O shepherds, whom have you seen?
Speak and tell us:
Who has appeared on earth?

SINGERS

(Stand and speak in unison.)

We saw a child in a manger!
We saw choirs of angels on high, praising the Lord!

NARRATOR

(Speaking more insistently.)

Tell us again:
What did you see?

SINGERS

(Speaking in unison, more loudly.)

We saw a child in a manger!
We saw choirs of angels on high, praising the Lord!

SINGERS and INSTRUMENTALISTS

(Singers, still standing, sing accompanied by Instrumentalists, who emphasize percussion for this carol. The Modern English metrical lyrics, translated below from the Latin "Feste dies agitur," should be sung to the music in *The New Oxford Book of Carols*. Use the stress patterns as indicated by the stems above the staff in the score in *The New Oxford Book of Carols*. After all three verses are sung, Instrumentalists continue playing the tune until Wassailers exit.)

"Feste dies agitur," #6 in *The New Oxford Book of Carols,* verses 1, 2, and 3.

Metrical lyrics, in Modern English, for carol #6:

1. Christmastime at last is here!
Our salvation brings us cheer,
Now the virgin's son appears
And fills the world with brilliant light.

Refrain: Our salvation brings us cheer!
Christ is born, our savior bright.

2. Let us cast away all fear!
Our salvation brings us cheer,
At the turning of the year
His birth dispels the dark of night.

Refrain: Our salvation brings us cheer!
Christ is born, our savior bright.

3. O how bless'd the virgin dear!
Our salvation brings us cheer,
As Mary did the angel hear,
A voice that came from heaven's height.

Refrain: Our salvation brings us cheer!
Christ is born, our savior bright.

WASSAILERS

(Enter from the lobby via the center aisle as soon as the Singers start to sing. The Wassailers frolic toward the stage and ascend the stage steps. They remove the cloth covering from the Wheel of Christmastide and turn the Wheel around several times, ending up with the arrow pointing to "26." They then descend the stage steps, divide up, and exit to the lobby via all aisles, carrying the cloth covering with them.)

READER

(Stands and reads distinctly and joyfully.)

Welcome Yule in best array,
In honor of the holy day!

Welcome be thou, heav'nly King!
Welcome, born on this morning!
Welcome to thee now we sing!
Welcome, Yule, forever and ay!
Welcome be ye, Stephen and John!
Welcome, Innocents, everyone!
Welcome, Becket, martyred one!
Welcome, Yule, forever and ay!
Welcome be thou, glad New Year!
Welcome, twelve days of good cheer!
Welcome, all ye that are here!
Welcome, Yule, forever and ay!

(END OF SEGMENT)

December 26 Segment
The Feast of St Stephen

Characters for This Segment

Singers, who sing as a group.
Instrumentalists, who accompany the Singers and provide sound effects. They should have a hand drum ready to play on cue.
Narrator, whose narration holds the segments together.
Reader, who reads passages from various medieval texts.
One Wassailer, who wears a Robin-Hood-style hat and turns the Wheel of Christmastide.
Stephen, the Christian Church's first martyr, who goes to his martyrdom stoically.
Rock Pelter A, Rock Pelter B, and Rock Pelter C, who mime the casting of their rocks at Stephen.

Setting and Props for This Segment

Ancient Jerusalem, the site of the stoning of Stephen, with no background scenery. The stage has general illumination; the audience is in darkness. If a spotlight is available, it can be used as noted. Props in this segment:

- three papier-mâché rocks, about 10-12 inches in diameter, painted gray
- Wheel of Christmastide, with the arrow pointing to "26," in place downstage left from previous segment

READER

(Stands at lectern.)

STEPHEN

(Enters solemnly stage left and stands downstage center.)

READER

From a sermon for December 26 by the 14th-century English priest John Mirk:

As the book of the deeds of the apostles tells us, after Christ was taken up into heaven, the apostles chose a few good, holy men from those who were Christ's disciples, to help in service to God. Of these, St Stephen was the first and the wisest. He was full of grace and of the power of the Holy Spirit, performing many wonders and miracles among the people. But, even if a man leads a very holy life, he will have enemies.

ROCK PELTERS A, B, and C

(Enter stage right, holding their rocks under their arms. While the Reader speaks, they look menacingly at Stephen and pretend to whisper to each other.)

READER

These enemies disputed with Stephen against the faith of Christ, with the purpose of overcoming Stephen in argument. By means of false witness, they wanted to condemn him to death. But Stephen was so full of the Holy Spirit that his enemies had no ability or power to withstand him. He openly overcame them in all matters, proving their arguments false. He was ready to accept death to verify all that he said.

The enemies of Stephen were even more angered against him, fretting in their hearts and grinding their teeth against him. And because they could not overcome him in disputation, they thought that they might accuse him of some words of slander against God, whereby they might have reason and cause to condemn him to death. Stephen knew about their malice, and he lifted his eyes unto heaven.

STEPHEN

(Looking upward, with hands raised.)

Lo, I see Jesus standing at his Father's right hand, ready to help me!

READER

And thereupon, Stephen's face shone with light, as if he were an angel of heaven.

STEPHEN and ROCK PELTERS A, B, and C

(Spotlight, if available, shines on Stephen, surrounded by the three Rock Pelters, now holding their rocks above their heads.)

READER

But when his enemies heard him speak thus, they cast him out of the city, to be stoned to death as a slanderer against God. And when they hurled stones at him, he cried out to God and said,

STEPHEN

(Folding his hands in prayer.)

Lord God, take my soul! Do not account this sin to them, but forgive them their sin.

INSTRUMENTALISTS

(Slow drum beats as Stephen and Rock Pelters depart.)

STEPHEN and ROCK PELTERS A, B, and C

(Still holding their rocks high above their heads, the three Rock Pelters walk Stephen down the stage steps and out the center aisle to the lobby, as a prisoner.)

READER

When St Stephen had said this, soon he fell asleep in God.

(Sits down.)

NARRATOR

(Stands at lectern.)

Yesterday, on Christmas, Christ descended to earth as the angels rejoiced.
Today Stephen ascends into heaven as he is stoned.

Yesterday the angels sang exultantly, "Glory to God in the highest."
Today they have joyously received blessed Stephen into their midst.

Yesterday Christ was wrapped up for us in swaddling clothes.
Today Stephen is clothed by Christ with the garment of immortality.

Yesterday the narrow manger held the infant Christ.
Today the boundless heavens receive the triumphant Stephen.

Our Lord descended all alone so that he might cause many to ascend.

(Sits down. If the audience is to sing along on the following carol, lights on the audience are turned on.)

SINGERS and INSTRUMENTALISTS

(Singers stand and sing in Modern English, accompanied by all Instrumentalists. If the audience is to sing along on this carol, an alternate Modern English translation may be used, as printed in the hymnals of many Christian denominations. After all the verses noted here are sung, Instrumentalists continue playing the tune until the Wassailer exits.)

"Of the Father's heart begotten," #19, version II, in *The New Oxford Book of Carols*, verses 1, 4, and 5.

ONE WASSAILER

(One Wassailer only enters from the lobby via the stage left aisle during the singing. The Wassailer walks in a dignified manner, ascends the stage steps, and turns the Wheel around twice, ending up with the arrow pointing to "27." The Wassailer then descends the stage steps and exits to the lobby via the stage right aisle.)

(END OF SEGMENT)

December 27 Segment
The Feast of St John the Evangelist

Characters for This Segment

Singers, who sing as a group.
Instrumentalists, who accompany the Singers.
Narrator, whose narration holds the segments together.
Reader, who reads passages from various medieval texts.
Wassailers, who wear Robin-Hood-style hats, turn the Wheel of Christmastide, and frolic up and down the aisles.
Pole Bearer, who walks in a stately manner, carrying the pole with the eagle banner.
John, disciple of Jesus and author of one of the Gospels, who is now a very old man.
Helper A, Helper B, and Helper C, who assist John as he walks.

Setting and Props for This Segment

Ancient Ephesus, with no background scenery. The stage has general illumination; the audience is in darkness. Props in this segment:

- simple wooden pole with a crosspiece at the top to hold a banner depicting an eagle
- Wheel of Christmastide, with the arrow pointing to "27," in place downstage left from previous segment

POLE BEARER

(Enters stage left, carrying the pole with the eagle banner, and walks slowly and solemnly to stand downstage left as the Reader begins reading.)

READER

(Stands at lectern to speak, taking care to avoid a singsong delivery of the poetry.)

From *The South English Legendary* of the late 13th century:

St John was well beloved of Christ, of all his friends the best.
He sat beside him and did lean upon the savior's breast.

JOHN and HELPERS A, B, and C

(While Reader is speaking, John, walking unsteadily and with great difficulty, enters stage right slowly. His Helpers hold him under each arm. They all end up standing downstage center.)

READER

At Christ's Last Supper when they ate, at ending of the day,
St John did wait upon the Lord and at his side did stay.

When on Good Friday Jesus Christ upon the cross did die,
His mother Mary and St John were always standing nigh.

Then into his own home and care St John this woman took.
Sweet Mary he did guard and tend, so says the holy book.

Now as an eagle John is shown, for high the eagle flies.
And eagles are the best of birds, and soar far in the skies.

And when an eagle is high up, where others cannot be,
He may still here upon the ground the smallest creature see.

St John was like an eagle then: his Gospel high began,
But also told of earthly life, of Jesus as a man.

(Sits down.)

NARRATOR

(Stands at lectern.)

St Jerome wrote in the 4th century:

When the holy evangelist John was living at Ephesus and was far advanced in years, his disciples would carry him into church. Since he was unable to give a lengthy sermon, at each gathering he was accustomed simply to speak these words:

JOHN

Children, love one another.

NARRATOR

His disciples and the brethren who were present, upon hearing these same words repeatedly, became impatient and asked him,

HELPER A

Master, why do you always say the same thing?

NARRATOR

John's reply was completely in harmony with his heart:

JOHN

Because it is the Lord's commandment.
And if you did nothing more, it would suffice.

JOHN and HELPERS A, B, and C

(Exit stage left, walking slowly.)

POLE BEARER

(Exits stage left, behind John and the Helpers, walking slowly.)

NARRATOR

St John is said to have lived for 68 years after the resurrection of Jesus, to about the age of 100.

(Sits down.)

SINGERS and INSTRUMENTALISTS

(Singers stand and sing in Modern English, accompanied by all Instrumentalists. Alternate Modern English translations of this carol can be found in the hymnals of many Christian denominations. After all the verses noted here are sung, Instrumentalists continue playing the tune until the Wassailers exit.)

"Unto us is born a son," #21, version II, in The New Oxford Book of Carols, verses 1, 3, and 5.

WASSAILERS

(Enter from the lobby via the side aisles during the singing. They interact with the audience members along the aisles as they frolic toward the stage. They ascend the stage steps, approach the Wheel of Christmastide, and turn the Wheel around several times, ending up with the arrow pointing to "28." They then descend the stage steps, divide up, and exit to the lobby via all aisles, again interacting with audience members.)

(END OF SEGMENT)

December 28 Segment
The Feast of the Holy Innocents

Characters for This Segment

Singers, who sing as a group.
Instrumentalists, who accompany the Singers.
Reader, who reads passages from various medieval texts.
Wassailers, who wear Robin-Hood-style hats and turn the Wheel of Christmastide.
Herod, the king of Judea, who wears a crown and carries a scepter. He is portrayed as an angry tyrant and was said to have ordered the slaughter of infants at the birth of Jesus.
Counselor A and Counselor B, who accompany Herod, each carrying a scroll.

Setting and Props for This Segment

Ancient Judea at the time of the birth of Jesus, with no background scenery. The stage has general illumination; the audience is in darkness. Props in this segment:

- scepter (hand-held wand with decorated ball at the tip)
- two scrolls (rolled-up strips of paper, each about a foot wide and two feet long); lines for Counselors A and B may be written on these scrolls
- Wheel of Christmastide, with the arrow pointing to "28," in place downstage left from previous segment

READER

(Stands at lectern.)

From a 13th-century sermon written in Kent, in southeast England:

We read in today's holy gospel that when our Lord God Almighty was born of the lady Mary in the city of Bethlehem, the star that announced his birth appeared to three kings in heathen lands in the East. By that star they knew about his birth, so they took counsel among themselves that they would travel to worship him.

And when they had prepared their offerings, the star went before them toward Jerusalem. There they spoke to Herod and asked him where they could find the one who was born king of the Jews. And when Herod heard that a king had been born who would be the king of the Jews, he, along with all of his counselors, was greatly displeased, because he feared that he would lose the kingdom of Jerusalem.

Then he summoned all the learned scholars who knew the Scriptures and asked them where Christ should be born. They answered, "In Bethlehem of Judea, for it was written and promised of old by the prophets." And when Herod heard this, he spoke to the three kings and said, "Go to Bethlehem and seek that child, and when you have found him, worship him. And afterwards come back to me, and I will go and worship him." Herod did not say this because he wanted to worship Christ but because he wanted to slay him if he could find him. The kings went on their way. And an angel from heaven appeared in a dream as they slept and commanded that they should not return to Herod but travel to their country by another route.

(Sits down.)

HEROD

(Rushing down the center aisle, shouting loudly and angrily, with Counselors A and B scurrying behind him. He speaks as he goes, ascending the stage steps to stand downstage center.)

O fie! O woe! O blast!
My anger and my spleen!
I fear those kings who passed,
Who here with me have been,
A web of lies have cast!
They promised to come clean
And tell me at the last
About the king they'd seen!

COUNSELOR A and COUNSELOR B

(Ascend stage steps as Herod speaks and stand on either side of him.)

HEROD

I tell you,
A boy they said they sought
With offerings they brought.
It moves my heart right naught
To break his neck in two!

Do tell me, Counselors,
What in your scrolls you find!

COUNSELOR A

(Consulting his scroll and speaking with authority.)

The prophecy is clear
To those who are not blind.
Isaiah tells it here:

It all has been designed.
A maiden without peer,
So clean in heart and mind,
        Shall him bear:
"Virgo concípiet
Natúmque páriet."
"Emmanuel" has yet
        His name to declare.

COUNSELOR B

(Consulting his scroll, nodding, and speaking with authority.)

In English we would say,
"Our God is with us" now.
The prophets point the way
To Bethlehem, I vow,
To a king in bright array
With crown upon his brow.
The Wise Men gone today
Shall find him there somehow.
        Lord of might!
And him shall honor
Both kings and emperors.

HEROD

(Still speaking angrily.)

Well, then, should I cower?
        Nay, you lie outright!

I never heard before
That a knave so slight
Should cause all this uproar
And rob me of my right!
I shall not stand for more!
This newborn king I'll smite!
I do declare a war
Upon this boy to fight!
        For I am stronger!
I swear by my crown,
I'll strike this lad down
In Bethlehem town
        Or I'll live no longer!

COUNSELOR B

(Speaking as if he's coming up with a great idea.)

The prophets tell it true,
What we all surely dread.
And Wise Men passing through
To Bethlehem have sped.
It's plainly up to you
To strike the boys all dead.
Each lad who's under two
Must quickly lose his head!
    In this way
The child you may kill
Thus at your own will.

HEROD

(Excitedly.)

His blood I will spill!
    I like what you say!

(Descends stage steps and stalks down center aisle to lobby.)

COUNSELORS A and B

(Descend stage steps behind Herod and exit down center aisle to lobby, looking at the scrolls and bantering with each other about their plans as they go.)

READER

(Stands at lectern.)

Now when the three kings had departed, behold an angel of the Lord appeared to Joseph in a dream and said, "Rise, take the child and his mother, and flee to Egypt, and remain there till I tell you. For Herod is about to search for the child, to destroy him." And Joseph rose and took the child and his mother by night and departed to Egypt.

(Sits down.)

SINGERS and INSTRUMENTALISTS

(Singers stand and sing, with quiet accompaniment by an instrument such as guitar or lute. Note that this carol works best if sung in the original Middle English and generally needs no translation because of its simple vocabulary. Singers may use Modern English pronunciation or may refer to "Pronunciation of

Fifteenth-Century English" in Appendix 1 of *The New Oxford Book of Carols*. After all the verses noted here are sung, Instrumentalists continue playing the tune until the Wassailers exit.)

"The Coventry Carol," #40 in *The New Oxford Book of Carols*, verses 1, 2, and 3.

WASSAILERS

(Enter from the lobby via the side aisles quietly and calmly during the singing. They ascend the stage steps, approach the Wheel of Christmastide, and turn the Wheel around several times, ending up with the arrow pointing to "29." They then divide up and exit the to the lobby via all aisles.)

(END OF SEGMENT)

December 29 Segment
The Feast of St Thomas Becket

Characters for This Segment

Singers, who sing as a group.
Instrumentalists, who accompany the Singers and provide sound effects. They should have a hand drum and cymbals ready to play on cue.
Narrator, whose narration holds the segments together.
Wassailers, who wear Robin-Hood-style hats, turn the Wheel of Christmastide, and frolic up and down the aisles, holding bird and animal masks up to their faces.
Thomas Becket, the archbishop of Canterbury, who wears his archbishop's miter. Becket was assassinated in the year 1170.
Knight A, Knight B, Knight C, and Knight D, each of whom carries a sword, assassinate Thomas Becket in Canterbury Cathedral.

Setting and Props for This Segment

Canterbury Cathedral in England, December 29, 1170, with no background scenery. The stage has general illumination; the audience is in darkness. Props in this segment:

- four long swords (can be made from stiff cardboard or thin plywood)
- Wheel of Christmastide, with the arrow pointing to "29," in place downstage left from previous segment

NARRATOR

(Stands at lectern.)

In the late 12th century, the archbishop of Canterbury, Thomas Becket, came into conflict with the king of England, Henry the Second, for a period of several years. The disputes concerned the authority of the king over certain functions of the church, such as how to judge clergy who were accused of crimes.

In December of the year 1170, rumors reached King Henry that Archbishop Becket was agitating against him and against the realm of England. King Henry expressed his continuing displeasure with the archbishop. Several knights in the king's court, hearing the king's angry words, decided to do the king a favor by assassinating the archbishop.

These knights secretly traveled to Canterbury on December 29. They found Becket in his cathedral, while he and his priests were saying their evening prayers. The priests tried to bar the door, but Becket opened it himself.

One eyewitness to the death of Becket was Edward Grim, who wrote this account of the events of December 29, 1170.

(Narrator sits down.)

READER

(Stands at lectern.)

BECKET

(Enters solemnly stage left and stands upstage left, hands folded in prayer.)

KNIGHTS A, B, C, and D

(Enter from the lobby, two down each of the side aisles, stomping as they walk and holding their swords up over their heads.)

KNIGHT A

(Loudly and angrily.)

Where is Thomas Becket, traitor to the king and to the realm of England?

BECKET

(Remains silent.)

KNIGHT B

(Even more angrily.)

Where is the archbishop?

BECKET

(Showing no fear, moving slowly to downstage center.)

Lo, here I am. I am no traitor to the king, but a priest.
What do you want from me?
Behold, I am ready to suffer in the name of Christ who redeemed me by his blood.
God forbid that I flee from your swords or depart from righteousness.

KNIGHTS A, B, C, and D

(All ascend the steps to the stage. Knights A, B, and C slowly circle around Becket many times, swords still held aloft, during the following exchange. Knight D stands to one side, as if keeping guard against interference.)

READER

The murderers pursued the archbishop, demanding repeatedly that he submit to King Henry's demands. Becket refused.

KNIGHT C

You shall die this instant and receive your just punishment!

BECKET

I am ready to die for my Lord, so that with my blood the church may obtain peace and liberty. But in the name of Almighty God, I forbid you to harm any of my men, whether clergy or laymen.

READER

At this rebuff, the knights were aflame with a terrible fury and brandished their swords against the archbishop's consecrated head. The archbishop understood that the hour was approaching that would release him from the miseries of this mortal life. Inclining his head as if in prayer, and joining his hands together and lifting them up, he commended his cause, and the cause of the church, to St Mary and to the martyr St Denis.

BECKET

(During this narration, Becket bows his head and lifts up his hands, as described by the Narrator.)

KNIGHTS A, B, C, and D

(All bend toward Becket, miming striking him with their swords. Knight D looks around, brandishing his sword, as if warding off anyone who might intervene.)

BECKET

(Crumples to the floor.)

INSTRUMENTALISTS

(As Becket falls, play a loud drum roll, followed by a crash of cymbals.)

KNIGHT D

Let us away! This fellow will rise no more!

KNIGHTS A, B, C, and D

(All descend the stage steps and exit to the lobby via the center aisle, quickly, with their swords pointed downwards. BLACKOUT: All lights, onstage and over the audience, go out briefly so that Becket can exit quickly and quietly, stage right.)

READER

(Reading with the light at the lectern.)

In all his sufferings, the martyr Thomas Becket displayed an astounding steadfastness. He did not oppose the fatal stroke either with his hands or with his robe. Nor did he say a single word when he was smitten. He did not utter either a cry or a groan or any sound indicating pain.

(Sits down.)

NARRATOR

(Stands at lectern.)

King Henry the Second did public penance at Becket's tomb, and many of the church privileges that Becket had argued for were granted. Three years later, in the year 1173, Becket was proclaimed a saint. The site of his martyrdom, Canterbury Cathedral, became a destination for holy pilgrimages by people from all over Europe.

(Sits down.)

SINGERS and INSTRUMENTALISTS

(Singers stand and sing in Modern English, accompanied by Instrumentalists. Singers' pronunciation on this carol should be very crisp. Note that this is the only musical piece in the pageant that is not found in *The New Oxford Book of Carols*. The tune is *Agincourt* ["O love, how deep, how broad, how high"], which can be found in the hymnals of most Christian denominations. See the **Guide to Staging** for more details. After all three verses below are sung, Instrumentalists continue playing the tune until the Wassailers exit at the end of the December 30 segment.)

"Song of St Thomas Becket," to the tune *Agincourt*

O hear ye now this wondrous tale
That we shall tell you without fail,
How Henry did the church assail
With wickedness he was incensed.

The greatest cleric in this land
Was slain by knights with evil hand.
While in his church he there did stand,
In Canterb'ry with no defense.

King Henry's knights with evil pride,
Before the altar him defied.
And there St Thomas bravely died.
They carried out this great offense.

WASSAILERS

(Enter from the lobby via the side aisles during the singing. They hold bird and animal masks, on sticks, in front of their faces and interact with the audience members along the aisles as they walk toward the stage. They ascend the stage steps, approach the Wheel of Christmastide, and turn the Wheel around several times, ending up with the arrow pointing to "30." They remain at the Wheel of Christmastide for the next segment.)

(END OF SEGMENT)

December 30 Segment
The Sixth Day in the Octave of Christmas

Characters for This Very Brief Segment

Singers, who sing as a group.
Instrumentalists, who accompany the Singers.
Wassailers, who wear Robin-Hood-style hats, turn the Wheel of Christmastide, and frolic up and down the aisles. They still hold their bird and animal masks.

Prop for This Very Brief Segment

- Wheel of Christmastide, with the arrow pointing to "30," in place downstage left from previous segment

WASSAILERS

(Looking thoughtfully at the Wheel of Christmastide and gesticulating, they go back and turn the Wheel again, this time ending up with the arrow pointing to "31." They then descend the stage steps, divide up, and exit to the lobby via all aisles, interacting with audience members.)

(END OF SEGMENT)

December 31 Segment
The Feast of St Sylvester

Characters for This Segment

Singers, who sing as a group.
Instrumentalists, who accompany the Singers.
Narrator, whose narration holds the segments together.
Wassailers, who wear Robin-Hood-style hats, turn the Wheel of Christmastide, and frolic up and down the aisles, distributing walnuts in shells from baskets.
Sylvester, who was a pope during the 4th century, wearing his papal triple tiara (three-tiered crown) and carrying a scythe.
Pole Bearer, who walks in a stately manner, carrying the pole with the triple-tiara banner.

Setting and Props for This Segment

Rome in the 4th century, with no background scenery. The stage has general illumination; the audience is in darkness. Props in this segment:

- simple wooden pole with a crosspiece at the top to hold a banner depicting a triple tiara
- scythe (can be made from stiff cardboard or thin plywood)
- three or four pounds of walnuts in shells
- small woven-wood baskets (may have bells attached; one basket for each of the Wassailers)
- Wheel of Christmastide, with the arrow pointing to "31," in place downstage left from previous segment

NARRATOR

(Stands at lectern.)

St Sylvester lived in the 4th century, during the reign of the Emperor Constantine the Great.

SYLVESTER

(Enters stage left, wearing his triple tiara and carrying a scythe, and walks slowly to stand downstage center while the Narrator speaks.)

POLE BEARER

(Enters stage left, following Sylvester, carrying the pole with Sylvester's triple tiara symbol on a banner, then stands to the side of Sylvester and slightly behind him.)

NARRATOR

Sylvester wears a triple tiara, to indicate that he is a pope. During his papacy, the declaration of Christian faith known as the Nicene Creed was written, at the Council of Nicea. In addition, several of the great churches of Rome were built.

Sylvester once wrote that, for Christians, every day should be holy. If we live with thoughts of eternity always before us, every day of the week can become a feast day, a holy day. Through the centuries, it was perhaps his observations about time that led to an association of Sylvester with "Father Time."

Sylvester died in the year 335. His feast day, December 31, falls on the last day of our calendar year. Carrying the traditional scythe, he ends the old year and ushers in the new year.

(Sits down.)

SYLVESTER

(Exits stage right, walking slowly.)

POLE BEARER

(Exits stage right, walking slowly, behind Sylvester.)

SINGERS and INSTRUMENTALISTS

(Singers stand and sing, accompanied by Instrumentalists, with emphasis on percussion such as tambourine during the refrains. This carol should be sung in the original languages, to preserve the mix of Latin and Middle English that was common in the late medieval period. Singers may use Modern English pronunciation or may refer to "Pronunciation of Fifteenth-Century English" in Appendix 1 of *The New Oxford Book of Carols*. A nonmetrical translation is provided in the **Program for Audience**, which precedes this script. After all the verses noted are sung, Instrumentalists continue playing the tune until the Wassailers exit.)

"Nowel syng we bothe al and som," #34 in from *The New Oxford Book of Carols*, verses 1, 3, and 5.

WASSAILERS

(Enter from the lobby via the side aisles during the singing, each carrying a small basket full of walnuts in shells. They pass out walnuts to audience members along the aisles as they frolic toward the stage. They ascend the stage steps, approach the Wheel of Christmastide, and turn the Wheel around several times, ending up with the arrow pointing to "1." They then divide up and exit to the lobby via all aisles, again interacting with audience members.)

(END OF SEGMENT)

January 1 Segment
The Feast of the Naming of Jesus, New Year's Day

Characters for This Segment

Singers, who sing as a group.
Instrumentalists, who accompany the Singers and provide sound effects. They should have two kazoos ready to play a mock fanfare on cue.
Reader, who reads passages from various medieval texts.
Wassailers, who wear Robin-Hood-style hats, turn the Wheel of Christmastide, and frolic up and down the aisles.
Arthur, a legendary king of Britain, who wears a crown.
Guinevere, Arthur's queen, who also wears a crown.
Arthur's Lords (minimum of three actors), who accompany Arthur. One Lord carries a couple of small fabric-wrapped boxes. Two of the Lords carry swords.
Guinevere's Ladies (minimum of three actors), who accompany Guinevere, each carrying a couple of small fabric-wrapped boxes.
The Green Knight, who is a giant puppet, surprising and somewhat fearsome, held aloft by a the Puppeteer. (See **Guide to Staging** for details.)
Puppeteer, who holds the Green Knight puppet aloft on cue.

Setting and Props for This Segment

King Arthur's court at Camelot, in a legendary British past, with no background scenery. The stage has general illumination; the audience is in darkness. Props in this segment:

- six small boxes, wrapped in solid fabric, representing New Year's gifts
- two long swords (can be made from stiff cardboard or thin plywood; these are two of the four swords that were used in the December 29 segment)
- Wheel of Christmastide, with the arrow pointing to "1," in place downstage left from previous segment

READER

(Stands at lectern.)

From the anonymous poem *Sir Gawain and the Green Knight* of the late 14th century:

King Arthur was at Camelot one Christmastide
With many courteous lords, the cream of his court,
All the gracious gathering of that grand Round Table.
With rich revelry and reckless mirth,
In tournaments time and time again,
These gentlemen knights jousted with jollity!

ARTHUR, GUINEVERE, ARTHUR'S LORDS, GUINEVERE'S LADIES

(Enter from the lobby down both side aisles, Lords carrying swords or boxes, Ladies carrying boxes. They mime animated conversation with each other, being careful not to make noise that would drown out the voice of the Reader. They should plan their entrance so that they arrive on the stage and stand downstage center before the Reader recites the words "Noel! Noel!")

READER

Then they convened with the court for singing of carols.
The feasting flowed full fifteen days,
With all the meats and merriment they could devise,
Gaily ringing glee, glorious to hear.
Such a fine din by day, such dancing at night!
All was high happiness in those chambers and halls,
With ample delights for each lord and lady.
King Arthur's friendly folk were lively and fresh,
Without care.

Most comely in their prime,
A people fine and fair!
This was the golden time;
None other could compare.

The old year had passed, the New Year was young,
So that day at the table the diners would be served double.
When the singing and psalms had ceased in the chapel,
King Arthur and his company came into the hall.
Both clerics and courtiers loudly called out.
"Noel! Noel!" was newly announced.

ARTHUR, GUINEVERE, ARTHUR'S LORDS, GUINEVERE'S LADIES

(All bow to each other, being jolly.)

Noel! Noel!

READER

The lords and ladies gave liberal largesse,
Granting New Year's gifts gladly, giving them by hand.

ARTHUR, GUINEVERE, ARTHUR'S LORDS, GUINEVERE'S LADIES

(Pass around boxes, bowing to each other and to Arthur and Guinevere.)

READER

But noble Arthur now proclaimed that he would never eat
On such a fair feast day until fully told
Of some unusual adventure as yet unheard;
Or of some amazing marvel that he might admire,
About exploits of ancestors or wars of great armies;
Or until a stranger should seek out a strong knight of his table
To join in jousting, to meet in jeopardy.
That was the king's custom when he held court
On each famous feast day with his followers
In his hall.

And so did Arthur stand,
So regal and so tall,
On New Year's as he'd planned
Over one and all.

INSTRUMENTALISTS

(Sound mock fanfare three times, on two kazoos.)

READER

Barely had the blasts of the trumpets abated
Heralding the first foods of the feast,

GREEN KNIGHT and PUPPETEER

(Enter stage left, breaking through the group of Lords and Ladies, who scatter in fright.)

READER

When there flung in at the door a fellow most fearsome,
The mightiest man, if you measured his stature,
From the throat to the thigh, thick-set and square,
With loins and limbs so long and so large
That he would be judged a giant on earth.
Yet mainly and mostly a man he seemed,
And the most handsome for his height that could ride on horseback.
What a scene!

All wondered at the hue
That on this knight was seen!
For plainly, through and through,
The knight was colored GREEN!

(Reader sits down.)

GREEN KNIGHT and PUPPETEER

(Slowly stride down the stage steps and out to the lobby via the center aisle.)

ARTHUR, GUINEVERE, ARTHUR'S LORDS, GUINEVERE'S LADIES

(Follow the Green Knight and the Puppeteer down the stage steps and out to the lobby via the center aisle, pointing their fingers and shaking their heads in disbelief.)

SINGERS and INSTRUMENTALISTS

(Singers stand and sing, accompanied by Instrumentalists, with emphasis on percussion such as tambourine during the refrains. This carol should be sung in the original languages, to preserve the mix of Latin and Middle English that was common in the late medieval period. Singers may use Modern English pronunciation or may refer to "Pronunciation of Fifteenth-Century English" in Appendix 1 of *The New Oxford Book of Carols*. A nonmetrical translation is provided in the **Program for Audience**, which precedes this script. After all the verses noted are sung, Instrumentalists continue playing the tune until the Wassailers exit.)

"Make we joye nowe in this fest," #31 in *The New Oxford Book of Carols,* verses 1, 2, 4, and 5.

WASSAILERS

(Enter from the lobby via the side aisles during the singing and frolic toward the stage, interacting with the audience along the way. They ascend the stage steps, approach the Wheel of Christmastide, and turn the Wheel around several times, ending up with the arrow pointing to "2." Looking thoughtfully at the Wheel of Christmastide and gesticulating, they go back and turn the Wheel again, this time ending up with the arrow pointing to "3." They then descend the stage steps, divide up, and exit the auditorium via all aisles, again interacting with audience members.)

(END OF SEGMENT)

January 2, 3, and 4 Segments
Weekdays (Feriae) of the Christmas Season

Characters for This Segment

Singers, who sing as a group.
Instrumentalists, who accompany the Singers.
Narrator, whose narration holds the segments together.
Wassailers, who wear Robin-Hood-style hats and turn the Wheel of Christmastide.
Mary, who is the calm mother of Jesus; she carries a large red fabric rose.

Setting and Props for This Segment

England, 15th century, with no background scenery. The stage has general illumination; the audience is in darkness. Props in this segment:

- oversized stemmed red rose, made from fabric
- Wheel of Christmastide, with the arrow pointing to "3," in place downstage left from previous segment

NARRATOR

(Stands at lectern.)

Mary, the mother of Jesus, was greatly revered in the Middle Ages as a guiding light for humanity. She was called the Queen of Heaven and the Star of the Sea. In this carol, she is compared to a perfect rose.

(Sits down.)

MARY

(Enters from lobby via left side aisle, carrying large red rose, as the Singers begin to sing. She walks silently and slowly toward the front of the auditorium, around the front of the audience, and back out the right side aisle to the lobby.

SINGERS and INSTRUMENTALISTS

(Singers stand and sing, with quiet accompaniment by one instrument—such as guitar, lute, hammered dulcimer, or soprano recorder. The Modern English metrical lyrics for this carol, below, can be sung to the music in *The New Oxford Book of Carols*. Alternatively, the Middle English and Latin lyrics in the carol book can be used. After all the verses noted are sung, Instrumentalists continue playing the tune until the Wassailers exit.)

"Ther is no rose of swych vertu," #28 in *The New Oxford Book of Carols,* verses 1, 2, 3, 4, and 5.

Alternate lyrics, in Modern English, for carol #28:

Refrain: There is no rose of such virtúe
As is the rose that bore Jesú.

1—There is no rose of such virtúe
As is the rose that bore Jesú.
Alleluia.
Refrain: There is no rose of such virtúe
As is the rose that bore Jesú.

2—For in this rose was Christ the Lord,
Him by all on earth adored.
O how wondrous.
Refrain: There is no rose of such virtúe
As is the rose that bore Jesú.

3—By that rose we may well see
There is one God in persons three,
Alleluia.
Refrain: There is no rose of such virtúe
As is the rose that bore Jesú.

4—Angels to the shepherds sang,
"Gloria" the heavens rang.
Let us rejoice.
Refrain: There is no rose of such virtúe
As is the rose that bore Jesú.

5—Let us leave this worldly mirth
And celebrate the joyous birth.
Alleluia.
Refrain: There is no rose of such virtúe
As is the rose that bore Jesú.

MARY

(Paces herself so that she is about to exit via the right side aisle to the lobby as the Wassailers enter.)

WASSAILERS

(Enter from the lobby via the left side aisle toward the end of the singing, with no frolicking, as Mary is departing toward the lobby via the right side aisle. The Wassailers ascend the stage steps, approach the Wheel of Christmastide, and turn the Wheel around several times, ending up with the arrow pointing to "4." Looking thoughtfully at the Wheel of Christmastide and gesticulating, they go back and turn the Wheel again, this time ending up with the arrow pointing to "5." They then descend the stage steps, divide up, and exit to the lobby via all aisles.)

(END OF SEGMENT)

January 5 Segment
Vigil of the Epiphany, Twelfth Night

Characters for This Segment

Singers, who sing as a group.
Instrumentalists, who accompany the Singers.
Narrator, whose narration holds the segments together.
Reader, who reads passages from various medieval texts.
Wassailers, who wear Robin-Hood-style hats, turn the Wheel of Christmastide, and frolic up and down the aisles, distributing walnuts in shells again.

Setting and Props for This Segment

England, 15th century, with no background scenery. The stage has general illumination; the audience is in darkness. Props used in this segment:

- walnuts in shells, left over from distribution at end of December 31 segment
- small woven-wood baskets (may have bells attached; one basket for each of the Wassailers)
- Wheel of Christmastide, with the arrow pointing to "5," in place downstage left from previous segment

READER

(Stands at lectern.)

A day made holy has dawned for us. Come, all ye nations, and adore the Lord. For today a great light has come down upon the earth. This is the day that the Lord has made. Let us be glad and rejoice in it.

(Sits down.)

NARRATOR

(Stands at lectern.)

Twelfth Night, the evening of January 5th, looks forward to the coming Feast of the Epiphany on January 6th.

In medieval England, Twelfth Night was the time to stoke up the last embers of the great Yule log in the family fireplace. On the evening of January 5th, groups of people went wassailing, singing at nearby houses and hoping to be rewarded with spiced drinks. They lit bonfires on the hillsides. They poured cider around the trees in their orchards, hoping to ensure a good harvest of fruit in the coming year.

(Narrator sits down.)

SINGERS and INSTRUMENTALISTS

(Singers stand and sing, accompanied by the Instrumentalists with plenty of percussion. The Modern English metrical lyrics for the stanzas of this carol, below, should be sung to the music in *The New Oxford Book of Carols*. The refrain should still be in Latin. A translation of the refrain is provided in the **Program for Audience**, which precedes this script. After all the verses noted are sung, Instrumentalists continue playing the tune until the Wassailers exit.)

"Gaudete," #51 in *The New Oxford Book of Carols,* verses 1, 2, and 4.

Lyrics, in Modern English, for carol #51, retaining Latin refrain:

Refrain: Gaudété, gaudété, Christús est nátus,
Ex María virginé: gaudété.

1—Now the time of grace is here,
Answer to our prayers.
Let us sing our songs of cheer,
Cast away our cares!
Refrain: Gaudété, gaudété, Christús est nátus,
Ex María virginé: gaudété.

2—God is born now as a child,
Yet king of all creation,
In a stable, meek and mild:
Marvel, all ye nations!
Refrain: Gaudété, gaudété, Christús est nátus,
Ex María virginé: gaudété.

4—Our assembled company,
Worship and adore him!
All of high and low degree,
Come and bow before him!
Refrain: Gaudété, gaudété, Christús est nátus,
Ex María virginé: gaudété.

WASSAILERS

(Enter from the lobby via the center aisle during the singing, each carrying a small basket full of walnuts in shells. They pass out walnuts to audience members along the center aisle as they frolic toward the stage. They ascend the stage steps, approach the Wheel of Christmastide, and turn the Wheel around several times, ending up with the arrow pointing to "6." They then descend the stage steps, divide up, and exit to the lobby via all aisles, again interacting with audience members.)

(END OF SEGMENT)

January 6 Segment
The Feast of the Epiphany

Characters for This Segment

Singers, who sing as a group.
Instrumentalists, who accompany the Singers and provide sound effects. They should have a hand drum ready to play on cue.
Reader, who reads passages from various medieval texts.
Wassailers, who wear Robin-Hood-style hats, turn the Wheel of Christmastide, and frolic up and down the aisles.
Joseph, who is the frazzled husband of Mary; he carries the wooden stool.
Mary, who is the calm mother of Jesus; she carries the wrapped doll.
Pole Bearer, who walks in a stately manner, carrying the star-topped pole.
Caspar, one of the Three Wise Men (Kings), who wears a crown and carries a small box that represents gold.
Melchior, one of the Three Wise Men (Kings), who wears a crown and carries a small box that represents frankincense.
Balthasar, one of the Three Wise Men (Kings), who wears a crown and carries a small box that represents myrrh.

Setting and Props for This Segment

The stable where Jesus is born, with no background scenery. The stage has general illumination; the audience is in darkness. Props in this segment:

- wooden stool, carried by Joseph to downstage center
- 18-inch doll wrapped in plain blanket, carried by Mary
- simple wooden pole with tin star (at least a foot across) affixed at the top, carried by Pole Bearer
- three small decorated boxes representing gold, frankincense, and myrrh, carried by Caspar, Melchior, and Balthasar respectively
- Wheel of Christmastide, with the arrow pointing to "6," in place downstage left from previous segment

READER

(Stands at lectern.)

The 4th-century Roman Prudentius wrote a poem that was celebrated throughout the Middle Ages:

O Bethlehem, greater than the greatest of cities, you have the honor of being the birthplace of Jesus, who is sent from heaven in human form to secure our salvation.

A star arose that outshone the sun in beauty and in brightness. The star announces the news: God has come to earth for the redemption of those on earth.

When the Wise Men see Jesus, they offer their gifts from the East. Bowing before him, they present gold, myrrh, and frankincense.

The precious gold proclaims that Jesus is a king. The sweet-scented frankincense shows that he is truly divine. And the myrrh foretells his tomb.

(Sits down.)

INSTRUMENTALISTS

(Play solemn drum beat for entrance of the Wise Men.)

CASPAR, MELCHIOR, and BALTHASAR

(Enter from lobby down the center aisle, processing regally to the drum beat from the Instrumentalists, holding their gifts before them. Caspar is carrying a box that represents gold, Melchior a box that represents frankincense, and Balthasar a box that represents myrrh.)

MARY, JOSEPH, and POLE BEARER

(Enter from stage left as the Wise Men start from the lobby. Mary is carrying the wrapped doll. Joseph is carrying the small wooden stool. The Pole Bearer is carrying the pole with a star on top. They take their places downstage center. Joseph places the stool on the stage, and Mary sits down on it. Joseph stands beside Mary, to her right. The Pole Bearer stands behind them both.)

CASPAR

(Approaches the stage and climbs the steps to stand to the left of Mary. As he begins to speak, he kneels.)

Hail, thou king, though poor and cold!
Hail, thou one so long foretold!
Hail, I come to thee with gold!
As writings do record,

On earth is gold the richest thing,
An off'ring fit for any king,
So here to thee this gold I bring,
To honor thee as Lord.

(Caspar places box of gold at the feet of Mary, then rises and steps back to stand by Pole Bearer, to allow Melchior to come forward.)

MELCHIOR

(Approaches the stage and climbs the steps to stand to the left of Mary. As he begins to speak, he kneels.)

O Lord, I kneel upon my knee.
Sweet incense here I offer thee!
Thou art our priest of high degree,
And none so great in might!

In God's own house, as all shall see,
We shall serve the Trinity,
One great God in persons three,
And all one Lord of might.

(Places box of frankincense at the feet of Mary, then rises and steps back to stand by Pole Bearer, next to Caspar, to allow Balthasar to come forward.)

BALTHASAR

(Approaches the stage and climbs the steps to stand to the left of Mary. As he begins to speak, he kneels.)

Lord, I kneel down by thy bed.
O maiden's son, I bow my head!
Thou wilt die in sinners' stead,
For our sins' relief.

Bitter myrrh here offer I
In token sure that thou wilt die
A bitter death of agony.
I make a cry of grief.

(Places box of myrrh at the feet of Mary, then rises and steps back to stand by Pole Bearer, next to Caspar and Melchior.)

MARY

O wise men and friends,
I thank and commend!
May God you defend
As homeward you wend!
Your kingdoms you'll tend
Until your lives end!

SINGERS and INSTRUMENTALISTS

(Singers stand and sing in Modern English, accompanied by all Instrumentalists. If the audience is to sing along on this carol, an alternate Modern English translation may be used, as printed in the hymnals of many Christian denominations. Also, if the audience is to sing along, lights on the audience are turned on. After the two verses noted here are sung, Instrumentalists continue playing the tune as the cast and crew assemble for bows. Once everyone is assembled, Instrumentalists stand for bows also.)

"On this day earth shall ring," #20 in *The New Oxford Book of Carols,* verses 1 and 3.

(END OF FINAL SEGMENT)

ALL CAST NOT ALREADY ONSTAGE and ALL TECHNICAL CREW

(Come out to the stage for bows.)

(END OF SCRIPT OF THE PAGEANT)

Resources Consulted

Note: All translations and paraphrases in the pageant are by the author of the pageant.

Breviarium ad usum insignis ecclesiae Sarum, edited by Francis Procter and Christopher Wordsworth. Cambridge University Press, 1882.

The Becket Controversy, edited by Thomas M Jones. John Wiley & Sons, 1970.

The Church's Year of Grace, Pius Parsch. Liturgical Press, 1964.

A Clerk of Oxford, aclerkofoxford.blogspot.com.

The Early English Carols, edited by Richard Leighton Greene. Oxford University Press, 1935.

Early English Christmas Carols, edited by Rossell Hope Robbins. Columbia University Press, 1961.

Early Middle English Verse and Prose, edited by JAW Bennett and GV Smithers, glossary by Norman Davis. Clarendon Press, 1968.

The Early South-English Legendary, edited by Carl Horstmann. Early English Text Society OS 87, 1887.

The English Hymnal with Tunes. Oxford University Press, 1933.

Ludus Coventriae or The Plaie called Corpus Christi, edited by KS Block. Early English Text Society ES 120, 1922.

Materials for the History of Thomas Becket, Archbishop of Canterbury, edited by James C Robertson. Rerum Britannicarum Medii Aevi Scriptores 67, volume 2, 1876.

The Medieval Christmas, Sophie Jackson. Sutton, 2005.

Middle English Dictionary, edited by Hans Kurath, Sherman Kuhn, Robert E Lewis, et al. University of Michigan Press, 1954-2001; also online.

Mirk's Festial: A Collection of Homilies by Johannes Mirkus, edited by Theodor Erbe. Early English Text Society ES 96, 1905.

New Catholic Encyclopedia, 1st edition, edited by William McDonald. McGraw-Hill, 1967-1996.

The New Oxford Book of Carols, edited by Hugh Keyte and Andrew Parrott, with associate editor Clifford Bartlett. Oxford University Press, 1992.

The Poems of John Audelay, edited by EK Whiting. Early English Text Society OS 184, 1931.

A Selection of English Carols, edited by Richard Leighton Greene. Clarendon Press, 1962.

Sir Gawain and the Green Knight, edited by I Gollancz. Early English Text Society OS 210, 1940.

The South English Legendary, edited by C d'Evelyn and AJ Mill. Early English Text Society OS 235, 236, and 244; 1956, 1959.

The Towneley Plays, edited by George England, notes and introduction by Alfred W Pollard. Early English Text Society ES 71, 1897.

York Plays: The Plays Performed by the Crafts or Mysteries of York on the Day of Corpus Christi, edited by Lucy Toulmin Smith. Russell and Russell, 1885.

Acknowledgments

Many thanks to Dorothy Devin for creating the cover art for *The Medieval Twelve Days of Christmas* and to Paul R Schwankl for his impeccable copyediting and formatting. Thanks also to the readers of drafts, who made numerous helpful comments: Josephine Tsai, Revd Stephen Sharman, Carol Richard, and Vera Schwankl.

An earlier version of *The Medieval Twelve Days of Christmas* was performed at St Thomas the Apostle Catholic Church in Ann Arbor, Michigan, in 2002. All the volunteers who contributed onstage or backstage to that production of the pageant deserve thanks for their great dedication and creativity: Mary Carol Fromes, Ann Rauen, Anne Schmidt, Brendon Schramm, Peter Schwankl, Vera Schwankl, Carol Dick, Bill Forgacs, Brian Neau, Garrett Schramm, Dorothy Schwankl, Tom Sponseller, Vicki Wozny, Paul R Schwankl, Glenn Smith, Madeleine Smith, Zach Norman, Barb Norman, Carol Richard, Abby Smith, Tina Shelcusky, Paul Malocha, Jesse Norman, Ken Norman, Lucas Norman, BJ Razgunas, John Schramm, Paula Miska, Ashley Riedlinger, Charlotte Smith, Joni Strickfaden, Lindsay Schramm, TV Silvia, John Norton, Darren Shelcusky, John Attarian, Elizabeth M Solsburg, Shirley Polakowski, Andrew Peltcs, Caroline Peltcs, Sharon Tewes (and all her sixth-grade and art students at St Thomas Elementary School in the 2001-2002 school year). Musician Gregory Hamilton brought the production to life with his lute playing. The late Revd Roger Prokop championed the production in the parish and then took on the role of Thomas Becket with amazing aplomb.

Cedar Park Press (CedarParkPress.com) has kindly been handling promotion for *The Medieval Twelve Days of Christmas* and would like to know about productions of this pageant around the world. Please share your staging experiences by emailing the press and the author at CedarParkPress@gmail.com. Photos and videos are most welcome!

About the Author

Karis Crawford holds a PhD in medieval literature from the University of Toronto, as well as a License in Medieval Studies from the Pontifical Institute of Medieval Studies. She served as an associate editor for the *Middle English Dictionary*, taught medieval and Renaissance literature at the University of Michigan, and led a graduate writing program at Hamline University. Her 2018 novel, *Adventures of a Girl Architect*, written under the pen name Hazel Harzinger, is also available on amazon.com. In 2002, Karis produced and directed a successful staging of *The Medieval Twelve Days of Christmas* in Ann Arbor, Michigan, for an audience of about 500. Watch for publication of her next musical pageant, *A Medieval Advent.*

Printed in Great Britain
by Amazon

50394372R00044